Leonard Whibley

Political Parties in Athens During the Peloponnesian War

Prince Consort Dissertation, 1888. Second Edition

Leonard Whibley

Political Parties in Athens During the Peloponnesian War
Prince Consort Dissertation, 1888. Second Edition

ISBN/EAN: 9783337078089

Printed in Europe, USA, Canada, Australia, Japan

Cover: Foto ©Suzi / pixelio.de

More available books at **www.hansebooks.com**

Cambridge Historical Essays. No. I.

POLITICAL PARTIES IN ATHENS

DURING THE

PELOPONNESIAN WAR.

BY

L. WHIBLEY, M.A.,

FELLOW OF PEMBROKE COLLEGE, CAMBRIDGE.

PRINCE CONSORT DISSERTATION, 1888.

SECOND EDITION.

Cambridge:

AT THE UNIVERSITY PRESS.

1889

Cambridge:

PRINTED BY C. J. CLAY, M.A. AND SONS,

AT THE UNIVERSITY PRESS.

PREFACE TO THE SECOND EDITION.

THE following dissertation was published at the beginning of this year in accordance with the terms under which the Prince Consort Prize is awarded. In preparing the second edition I have made few changes of importance.

The subject was originally chosen by myself and approved by the Adjudicators. The purpose I have kept in view is to describe the state of politics and political parties in Athens, without discussing the separate and successive events of political history. Certain questions, which do not directly bear on the history of politics, are treated at some length, either on account of the intrinsic interest of those questions or on account of the obscurity in which they are involved.

A list of the chief modern historians whose works I have consulted is prefixed; I have also quoted in the notes the source from which important suggestions or conclusions have been derived. In particular I wish to acknowledge how much I am indebted to Dr BELOCH, whose work "Die attische Politik seit Perikles" contains a most able discussion of the political life of Athens.

In preparing my dissertation for publication I had the advantage of many criticisms and suggestions from Mr R. A. NEIL of Pembroke College, to whom I offer my heartiest thanks.

L. WHIBLEY.

PEMBROKE COLLEGE, CAMBRIDGE,
November, 1889.

CONTENTS.

LIST OF THE CHIEF MODERN WORKS
QUOTED AND CONSULTED.

Beloch (J.), Die attische Politik seit Perikles.

Die Bevölkerung der griechisch-römischen Welt.

Zur Finanzgeschichte Athens (in the Rheinisches Museum, xxxix. 1884).

Böckh (A.), Die Staatshaushaltung der Athener (Dritte Auflage herausgegeben von Max Fränkel).

Büchsenschütz (B.), Besitz und Erwerb im griechischen Alterthume.

Curtius (E.), The History of Greece (translated by A. W. Ward).

Droysen (J. G.), Bemerkungen über die attischen Strategen (in Hermes, ix).

Fränkel (M.), Die attischen Geschworenengerichte.

Freese (W. L.), Der Parteikampf der Reichen und der Armen in Athen.

Gilbert (G.), Beiträge zur innern Geschichte Athens im Zeitalter des peloponnesischen Krieges.

Handbuch der griechischen Staats-alterthümer. Erster Band.

Grote (G.), A History of Greece (the edition of 1870 in 12 volumes).

Hertzberg (G. F.), Alkibiades.

Kirchhoff (A.), De Republica Atheniensi (in the Abhandlungen der k. Pr. Akademie, Berlin 1878).

Köhler (U.), Urkunden und Untersuchungen zur Geschichte des delisch-attischen Bundes (ib. 1869).

Müller-Strübing (H.), Aristophanes und die historische Kritik.

Der Staat der Athener (in Philologus, Supplementband iv.).

Oncken (W.), Athen und Hellas. Zweiter Band.

Scheibe (K. F.), Die oligarchische Umwälzung zu Athen am Ende des peloponnesischen Krieges.

Vischer (W.), Kleine Schriften. Erster Band.

Wilamowitz-Möllendorff (U. von), Philologische Untersuchungen i., Aus Kydathen.

INTRODUCTION.

In the history of Athens the period of the Pelo- *The period of the Pelopon- nesian war.* ponnesian war deserves and admits of special atten- tion. Not only have we fuller materials, scanty as these are, for this epoch than for any other part of Athenian history, but the period has a unity and an interest of its own. The years before are differentiated by the ascendency of Pericles, which overshadowed the ordinary forces of politics; the years succeeding 404 show us Athens completely transformed by the struggles and sufferings she had gone through; and finally the war itself was of critical and decisive importance, for all states of Greece were involved in it[1], and the history of Athens is for the time not the history of a single commonwealth but broadens into the history of all Greece.

Herein lies the historical importance of the period, and on this account the political movements, the composition and organization of parties, the subjects on which they were divided, and the policy they pursued possess an interest greater than usually attaches to political history.

---

[1] Thuc. i. 1, emphasizes its importance in this respect.

W.   1

*Inade-
quacy and
bias of the
original
authori-
ties.*   But if the study of Athenian politics in this
period has special importance, it has also special
difficulties. The original authorities for political
events are very inadequate, and this deficiency of
original materials has led to the multiplication of
modern works, since the absence of certain information leaves a wide field to be filled up according to
the views of individual writers. Hence the most
widely divergent and even contradictory theories find
supporters, and between these theories it is sometimes impossible to decide. Our investigations often
fail to attain to any positive result, and many questions remain in the realm of complete uncertainty or
at best of mere probability.

Besides the deficiency of available materials there
is another general characteristic of the original
authorities which must not be left out of view. The
bias, which must have influenced them in writing
on political events, is variously estimated, and this
is largely responsible for the differences of modern
writers.

*Old view of
Athenian
politics.*   The old school of historians represented by Böckh
and K. F. Hermann, and caricatured by Mitford,
accepting without question the blame cast on the
democracy by ancient writers, and in some cases
intensifying it, passed on it a verdict almost wholly
unfavourable. While Pericles obtained from most of
this school almost more than his due meed of praise,
the people he had led and those leaders who followed
in his footsteps were visited with condemnation.
The people as well as the demagogues lacked every
political virtue and committed every political fault.

Grote employed a new method, which led to new *Grote and*
conclusions. No contemporary authority must be *later writers.*
implicitly trusted without allowing for the political
sympathies and antipathies he entertained. This
critical treatment threw a new light on political
questions, and led to a revision of the former verdict.
Conclusions favourable to democracy were deduced,
conclusions which were coloured by Grote's own
enthusiasm. The effect of his work has been permanent, no later historian has been able to dis-
regard it: many have accepted his views and extended their application[1]; others have disagreed with
many of his conclusions, but have had to justify
their dissent by sounder arguments than had been
hitherto accepted. The present tendency leans to
a more moderate estimate of Athenian democracy,
less unfavourable than that of the early school, but
not so enthusiastic as that of Grote[2].

The uncertainty of our conclusions on political *Bias of*
subjects, which is due to the inadequacy and bias of *the au-*
the original authorities, requires us to review those *thorities*
authorities, with especial reference to these two points. *against de-*
At the outset it must be admitted that they are *mocracy.*
in the main unfavourable to the democracy[3]. Our
histories all come from one side, and scarcely give
us more than half the truth; at best the leading
democrats have to be whitewashed[4], and it is im-

[1] e.g. Oncken, and in the main Müller-Strübing.

[2] Beloch and Gilbert are representatives of this tendency.

[3] This is true not only of the historians but of the poets
and philosophers, such as Aristophanes, Euripides, Plato and
Socrates.

[4] As Cleon has been by Grote. Oncken, Athen und Hellas, ii.

possible to realize how far we should have to revise
our conclusions, if any work written from the democratic standpoint had come down to us.

Thucy-
dides.

Of all authorities Thucydides is by far the most
important, but this is because the other authorities
are so lamentably meagre. Thucydides was not
writing the history of a period, but of an event,
the Peloponnesian war. He carefully avoids home
politics[1], and leaves out of view all subjects which
were not more or less closely connected with the
causes and progress of the war. Hence, except in
the eighth book, we get but little light on politics
from Thucydides, and Müller-Strübing[2] is justified
in asking—"Is there another representation of the
history of a period, written by an able, well in-
structed contemporary, from which we get so little
definite information on constitutional development,
political party struggles, the motives of the events
described, intellectual movements or the inner life of
the people ?"

p. 205, says that the only reference to him in ancient writers
which is not unfavourable is in Plut. Praec. reip. ger. 13. To
this we may perhaps add Dem. 40, 25, where he is referred to
without depreciation or apology as an eminent general.

[1] Among important events not mentioned by Thucydides are
the raising of the tribute in 425, the raising of the dicast's fee, the
ostracism of Hyperbolus (only incidentally referred to at a later
date). His account of affairs after the mutilation of the Hermae
is very confused, and his description of the measures taken after
the Sicilian expedition is exceedingly indefinite.

[2] Aristophanes, p. 386. It is true that the speeches in Thucydides, whatever view be taken of their authenticity, throw great
light on the political ideas of his time; but even when he does
describe some important debate, he does not usually distinguish
the political parties by name.

We are on more dangerous ground in discussing the bias of Thucydides: with some writers it has been the fashion to accept everything that Thucydides wrote, almost as if he were verbally inspired; but even in his case personal prejudice must have had an unconscious effect[1]. His known aristocratic sympathies and his condemnation by the democracy are sufficient to account for his bias, which appears in his favourable judgment of Antiphon[2], compared with his description of Hyperbolus[3], as well as in the severe condemnation of Cleon[4], which is not justified by his own account of that demagogue. As Oncken[5] says, we may implicitly trust Thucydides for statements of fact, but must exercise our own judgment in criticizing his comments on events.

Xenophon takes up the history where Thucydides *Xenophon.* leaves off. He gives a full account of the trial of the generals in 406 and of the break-up of the rule of the Thirty, but both accounts are coloured by the most extreme prejudice; and his contributions to the history of politics (and there are scarcely more than these) are as far below those of Thucydides, as he himself is inferior as an historian.

Aristophanes is of far greater importance, but we *Aristo-* get little more from him than isolated references to *phanes.*

---

[1] A. Schmidt quoted by Müller-Strübing, ib. p. 482, says, "The man who thinks Thucydides impartial is in error. Theopompus' partiality was gross and evident, but Thucydides' is so carefully concealed, that we can only discover it with immense trouble and luck."

[2] viii. 68.　　　　　　　　[3] viii. 73.

[4] He sums up his career in v. 16, but he never mentions him without some unfavourable description. iii. 36, iv. 28, 39.

[5] Athen und Hellas, ii. p. 231.

single characters or events. Even these must be
received with great caution. His political views
made him an opponent of the extreme democrats,
and the antagonism was embittered by personal feeling, for we are told of at least three occasions, on
which Cleon attacked the poet or his representative[1].
But apart from his political prejudices, he was, as a
comic poet, not bound by any canons of historical
truth[2]. In his representation of public men Aristophanes employs paradox as frequently as exaggeration. Hence there are many passages in which we
must interpret him by contraries; in particular I
think that this interpretation serves to explain
many details of Cleon's character in "the Knights."

His treat-   It has been pointed out[3] that Cleon, as he appears
ment of   in Aristophanes, differs essentially from the picture
Cleon.   that we have of him in Thucydides. For the
passionate orator, overawing the people, who appears
in the pages of the historian, the poet has substituted
a cringing flatterer and servant of the Demos. This
opposition can be traced in detail throughout the
play. Thus Cleon is charged with neglect of military
duty ($\dot{a}\sigma\tau\rho a\tau\epsilon\acute{\iota}a$)[4], a reproach appropriate enough in
Cleon's mouth against Nicias, but absurd as applied
to the victor of Pylus: he is charged with plotting
with the Spartans[5], another paradox, when we remember that in the year before he had objected to

---

[1] The first three plays of Aristophanes were brought out in the
name of Callistratus, against whom, therefore, Cleon's first attack
must have been directed. Müller-Strübing, ib. p. 72.

[2] See Müller-Strübing, ib. pp. 3 and 5.

[3] By Oncken, ib. p. 226.

[4] 443.   [5] 465.

treating with them at all: again he is charged with
receiving bribes from Mytilene[1], an impossibility
when we remember the sentiments Thucydides puts
into his mouth in the debate on the treatment of
Lesbos, but a charge actually made by Cleon against
his opponents[2]: lastly with advocating peace[3]. When
we consider that many of these charges have been
laboriously explained by scholiasts, both ancient and
modern, as referring to actual incidents in Cleon's
career, it is worth while pointing out that the poet
is simply turning against Cleon charges which the
demagogue constantly brought against his opponents.✓
These gained their piquancy from their very in-
appropriateness to him, and we may conclude that
we have here to deal not with exaggeration but with
paradox.

Aristophanes' treatment of public men may be
tested in cases where we have other evidence. He
condemns Pericles[4], though not so severely as he
does Cleon; but every one now rejects his authority
in the case of Pericles, because that statesman is
redeemed by the testimony of Thucydides[5]. It is

*His treat-
ment of
Pericles.*

---

[1] 834.   [2] Thuc. iii. 38.

[3] 669.

[4] See passages quoted in the next note. In Vesp. 715, which
apparently refers to Pericles, no distinction is drawn between him
and the other demagogues; but in Eq. 191, 283 he is favourably
contrasted with Cleon.

[5] Hermann, Staatsalterthümer, § 164, is strikingly illogical.
After quoting Aristophanes (Ach. 525, Pax 605) on Pericles, he
admits "it would be partial to ascribe such views to Pericles,"
but immediately afterwards he gives an unfavourable description
of the later demagogues, the details of which are unsupported
except by isolated references to Aristophanes.

obvious that Aristophanes' treatment of Cleon is of no more value, as a piece of impartial evidence. From these reasons it will be seen that it is necessary to use Aristophanes for historical purposes with the utmost care. We may accept the rule laid down by Vischer[1]—" For the judgment of individual character, for the discovery of single facts, we must regard the old comedy as an entirely unreliable authority, which can only be justified in connection with other sources, and not always then."

The work on the Athenian Constitution. A valuable contribution to our knowledge of the Athenian democracy and empire, as well as a most trenchant criticism of it, is contained in the work on the Athenian Constitution, which was for a long time ascribed to Xenophon. The view that it came from his pen is now generally given up, and although the authorship cannot be determined, there is good reason for fixing the date at which it was produced between 424 and 414[2]. It has, therefore, exceptional value from the fact that it was written at a time before the Athenian power had suffered any grave diminution, and lacks the morbid sense of its defects, which were subsequently regarded as the causes of disaster.

---

[1] Kleine Schriften, i. p. 184.

[2] Kirchhoff (Abhand. der Akad. Ber. 1878, pp. 1—24), ascribes it to the former date, as he thinks it must have been written before Brasidas' march to Thrace. Müller-Strübing (Philologus, Supplementband iv. p. 74), dismissing this consideration, thinks 415 the most likely date. He sees in the work the attempt of an extreme oligarch to combine the different sections of the oligarchical party in a common policy against the constitution. He thinks the tone of the work is consistent with what we know of Phrynichus, whom he concludes to be the author.

Throughout the work there is a contrast between *The political standpoint of the writer.* what the author regards as the ideally best con- stitution[1]—oligarchy, and the constitution which Athens had adopted—democracy. To him oligarchs are χρηστοί[2], democrats πονηροί, and the Athenian constitution favours the base at the expense of the good. His fondness for oligarchy is carried so far that in his eyes the possession of oligarchic sym- pathies is equivalent to virtue and wisdom[3], men of his party are οἱ βέλτιστοι, in all states τὸ βέλτιστον is ἐναντίον τῇ δημοκρατίᾳ[4], and εὐνομία[5] according to his standard would involve the over- throw of democracy and the enslavement of the people. These quotations will suffice to show the extreme and undisguised prejudice, which he en- tertains for oligarchy, and which deprives his work of all claim to judicial criticism ; but he also shows clearly enough that granting the imperfections of democracy, the Athenians pursue the end most desirable for[6] themselves, i.e. to be free and rule[7], and take the best means to preserve the con- stitution[8]. I have discussed the standpoint of the writer at some length, because I shall have occasion to refer to his opinions again, and it will be useful to remember then that he is no friend to the democracy.

---

[1] i. 8.

[2] i. 1. These terms βέλτιστοι, χρηστοί, πονηροί are all used in their quasi-political sense.

[3] i. 7.   [4] i. 5.   [5] i. 9.

[6] i. 6. ὁ...πονηρὸς ἐξευρίσκει τὸ ἀγαθὸν αὐτῷ τε καὶ τοῖς ὁμοίοις αὐτῷ.

[7] i. 8.   [8] i. 1.

Lysias and Andocides. The other authorities may be briefly dismissed. Lysias and Andocides give us a certain amount of information on political events, the latter being especially useful for the years 415, 410, 404–3.

Aristotle, Plutarch and Diodorus. Coming to authors who were not contemporary, we find Aristotle's contributions of no very definite value. Most of his statements are general, and even when he evidently has Athens in view, his criticism is often more appropriate to his own age than to the earlier period[1]. Plutarch and Diodorus add little to our knowledge; we are indebted to them for some information, which they derived from authors, whose works are now no longer extant. Of these the most important were Ephorus and Theopompus. The difficulty of criticism is increased, when we get the authorities only at second hand.

Inscriptions. I have now discussed the materials of direct historical importance, with the exception of inscriptions. On constitutional points these often give us valuable information, but they are far from filling up the deficiencies of our authors. I have endeavoured to show that our only extant historians, Thucydides and Xenophon, give us absolutely no information on many political events, so that we often have to rely on non-historical writers, orators, philosophers and poets; and that even from the sum of all these materials we cannot get a continuous history of politics.

---

[1] Aristotle was not favourable to extreme democracy (Pol. 1312 b, 5). His ideal was a μέση πολιτεία and according to Plutarch (Nic. 2) his favourite statesmen were Thucydides, Nicias and Theramenes, men of moderate views.

The consequence is that politics in Athens ap- *No con-
pear to us in a series of dissolving views: some few *tinuous history of*
events can be clearly understood, but we are generally *politics.*
left to our own resources for the causes and consequences of them. It is the same with the actors
on the political stage. Some few men stand out
vividly before us; Thucydides and Aristophanes
together enable us to realize Pericles, Cleon and
Nicias: but other characters must have played a part
of hardly less importance, and they appear to us only
once or in one scene. To take an example, what
part did Diodotus take in Athenian politics? We
may conclude from his one appearance in Thucydides,
that he was not only a statesman of ability but in all
probability the leader of the moderate party at this
juncture[1], but we never hear of him again. Who
was Thudippus who proposed the most important
financial measure in this period, the increase of the
tribute in 425[2]? We only know of his existence
from the inscription containing his proposal, and yet
he must have been a prominent member of his party
to be entrusted with so important a duty. The case
is the same with Demostratus[3] who proposed the
enrolment of forces for the Sicilian expedition, with
Thessalus[4] who prosecuted Alcibiades, and with many
others.

Nor is our knowledge of institutions and events *Uncer-*
more satisfactory. The absence of any account of *tainty on constitu-tional*

[1] Thuc. iii. **41 ff.** The words ὅσπερ καὶ ἐν τῇ προτέρᾳ ἐκκλησίᾳ *points.*
ἀντέλεγε κ.τ.λ. point to his having taken the lead on this occasion.

[2] C. I. A. i. 37.

[3] Ar. Lysist. 391.

[4] Plut. Alc. 22.

the constitution at this period admits of the widest difference of opinion on constitutional points. To take a few instances: some historians have developed a theory of the constitution in which the premiership is held by a state treasurer[1], whom other authorities will not allow to exist; another historian[2] has argued with great ability that there was absolutely no change in the laws between 460 and 411, and this theory, while it lacks sufficient confirmation to be accepted, cannot be satisfactorily disproved. These are typical cases, and it would be easy to cite many others, in which directly contradictory opinions are maintained between which it is impossible to decide[3].

Uncertainty on the subject of political parties. This uncertainty and difference of opinion are equally manifest on the subject of political parties. Original authorities give us little definite information on the division of parties, on their policy, or on the political standing of prominent men. Hence there results a great confusion of ideas; some modern historians talk of two parties, others of three; and the same men are variously described as aristocrats, oligarchs and democrats. It is only possible to ob-

---

[1] Müller-Strübing's great theory of the ταμίας τῆς κοινῆς προσόδου. Böckh, i. p. 200, regarded this officer as the head of Athenian finance. Most historians believe that this office was not instituted before Euclides.

[2] Wilamowitz, Aus Kydathen, p. 52, thinks that there was no process of legislation in this period.

[3] Some are discussed below, see pp. 20, 64 n. 2, 69 n. 1, 122 n. 1. In particular we have no evidence to determine whether institutions, known to exist in the fourth century, were part of the constitution before the archonship of Euclides, e.g. the νομοθέται and ἐπιχειροτονία.

tain more definite conceptions by realizing as far as possible the conditions of political life at Athens, and the motives of political action; on this account it is necessary to discuss the Athenian constitution and the Athenian empire in so far as they directly concern the study of politics, while we may neglect details indifferent to this purpose.

CHAPTER I.

The Athenian Constitution and Empire.

Necessity of democracy in Athens.
THE Athenian constitution was an extreme democracy, and it was impossible that it should be otherwise. The internal history of Athens, the policy of her statesmen, the influence of events in Greece, contributed to make this the only form of government possible, while it was certainly the only form which corresponded to her highest interests.

Aristotle[1] admits that in a large city any other form of constitution than democracy is an anomaly. The history of Athens in the fifth century is the history of her rise as a commercial and maritime power, and it is unnecessary to argue that in Greece there was a close connection between democracy and sea power and trade[2].

This tendency, which was at first natural, was fostered by her statesmen; Pericles and Themistocles directed their efforts to make Athens exclusively a sea power, and the attention paid to her fleet and

---

[1] Pol. 1286 b, 20, ἐπεὶ δὲ καὶ μείζους εἶναι συμβέβηκε τὰς πόλεις ἴσως οὐδὲ ῥᾴδιον ἔτι γίνεσθαι πολιτείαν ἑτέραν παρὰ δημοκρατίαν.

[2] See Müller-Strübing, Aristophanes, p. 82. Cf. Aristot. ib. 1304 a, 22, ὁ ναυτικὸς ὄχλος κ.τ.λ. Resp. Ath. i. 2.

fortifications rendered the city almost an island[1]. While internal circumstances demanded this constitution, the position of Athens in Greece had an equally strong influence in this direction. I shall endeavour to prove below that the confederacy of which Athens was the head was held together by community of democratic feeling and interest, and that on this account democracy was necessary to maintain the alliance. We see in the history of this period that democracy was for Athens a state of stable equilibrium; any disturbance of this could be only temporary and was always followed by a return to the former state. It was impossible even to introduce a less extreme form of democracy; a moderate democracy is only possible as a step in development, but cannot be artificially created from an extreme democracy[2].

The Athenian constitution rested on the two principles of freedom and equality[3]. Speech and opinion were free, and all citizens were equal before the law. From this equality of the citizens it resulted

Principles of Athenian democracy.

---

[1] Resp. Ath. ii. 14. Thuc. i. 143, Attica falls short of being an island in only one particular—the liability to ravages.

[2] Resp. Ath. iii. 8, 9. The lines of Aristophanes referring to Alcibiades (Ranae 1431) may be referred appropriately enough to such a constitution,

οὐ χρὴ λέοντος σκύμνον ἐν πόλει τρέφειν,
ἢν δ' ἐκτραφῇ τις, τοῖς τρόποις ὑπηρετεῖν.

[3] The principles of ἐλευθερία and ἰσονομία (cf. Oncken, Athen und Hellas, ii. p. 41). Thuc. iii. 82 (ἰσονομία πολιτική is the democratic watchword). Dem. Mid. 124 talks of ἰσηγορία and ἐλευθερία as the birthright of Athenians. The speech of Pericles (Thuc. ii. 37), discussing the constitution, dwells on τὸ ἴσον and τὸ ἐλεύθερον.

that the majority had absolute control of the government, for all power was vested in the citizen body assembled in the ἐκκλησία, where every question was decided by a majority of votes, without check or appeal[1].

All power exercised by the people. The people had all powers of government, and exercised them either directly or indirectly. The only apparent exception is in respect to judicial duties, which were surrendered to the dicasts, the only magistrates who were irresponsible[2], and whose action was not subject to appeal. But potentially and in theory every Athenian citizen of mature age was a dicast[3] (though all did not choose to exercise their right), so that the decisions of the courts were regarded as those of the people. Legislative, executive and deliberative powers were also not directly exercised by the public assembly, but here the people retained the right of ultimate control. Legislation was in the main conducted by a standing board (of νομοθέται)[4], subject to the approval of the assembly in each case. The executive power was in part surrendered to boards of magistrates, but the assembly, besides directing the executive, appointed the magistrates, and exercised the most jealous control over them, being competent to suspend them at any time[5],

[1] The establishment of the πρόβουλοι in 413 with a power of veto was such a check.

[2] Ar. Vesp. 587.

[3] This is Fränkel's theory (Die Attischen Geschworenengerichte, p. 20), 'Jeder Athener über dreissig Jahre von selbst Heliast war.'

[4] Supposing the νομοθέται existed before 411, a point in dispute, see above, p. 12 n. 3.

[5] If ἐπιχειροτονία existed in the 5th century.

and compelling them to render a strict account of
their office.

The council (βουλή), it is true, had extensive *Powers of the council.*
powers both administrative and executive ; it formed
a committee of public safety, meeting every day, and
performed duties for which the assembly was unfitted by its size, such as the transaction of current
business and the discussion of details. Hence the
council prepared all matters to go before the assembly, which accepted, rejected or amended the
proposals. This constituted its importance as a
deliberative body, but it had besides independent
functions of considerable extent. It saw to the
execution of the decrees passed by the assembly and
controlled the magistrates; it watched over the
military and naval forces of the state and managed
the business of the Athenian confederation ; lastly it
formed the most important financial authority, super-
intending the budget of the year and raising the
necessary funds.

From this varied activity the council attained
a certain importance, and was the special sphere of
many politicians, but from the fact that its members
were chosen by lot and from its real subordination
to the assembly its political powers were never really
great. From its constant meetings, its comparatively
small numbers, as well as from the fact that its
members sat for a year, it must have had great influence on the administration; but on important
questions of policy the real decision lay with the
sovereign assembly, and the council had simply to
anticipate or to follow its wishes.

Direct powers of the assembly.   As with the council, so with the other branches of government ; the assembly retained the ultimate decision and control, even when it delegated its authority. But for the consideration of party politics, the direct powers of the assembly are more important. Its action in all departments of state business was supreme and omnipotent : in theory it was supposed always to be in submission to the law of the constitution[1], but in course of time the belief gained ground that the demos was infallible, and the assembly overrode or suspended the laws, and realized that extreme development described by Aristotle in which " decrees are sovereign and not the law[2]." This direct supremacy of the assembly, in which every one had an equal voice and vote, and the most important question was irrevocably decided by a bare majority, made the Athenian constitution at once the most extreme and the most real democracy which has ever existed.

Powers of the magistrates.   The omnipotence of the assembly tended to reduce the magistrates also to a dependent position ; but just as the dicasts and the council were entrusted with some independent powers, so in financial and military matters there were magistrates possessed of

---

[1] The theory prevailed that the laws were sacred and eternal. Cf. Wilamowitz, Aus Kydathen, p. 3 and p. 47. The γραφὴ παρανόμων was introduced to prevent change except under the most rigid precautions.

[2] Pol. 1292 a, 4, ἕτερον εἶδος δημοκρατίας...κύριον δ' εἶναι τὸ πλῆθος καὶ μὴ τὸν νόμον. τοῦτο δὲ γίνεται ὅταν τὰ ψηφίσματα κύρια ᾖ ἀλλὰ μὴ ὁ νόμος. Andoc. 1. 87 points to decrees having overridden laws during the Peloponnesian war. Wilamowitz, ib. (pp. 54, 57) points out that the Athenians inflicted the greatest injuries on themselves by breaking down legal restraints, as in 415, 411, 406.

real authority. Most magistracies were filled up by means of the lot ; and this method, while it required the duties to be such as could be undertaken by the average citizen, deterred men of eminence from offering their services ; while conversely, the chief elective offices involved important functions and were keenly competed for. Thus the board of Helleno-tamiae transacted considerable financial business, and as a consequence we find leading Athenians serving on it[1]. But this magistracy involved more trust than power, and so was not the object of political contention in the same way as that of the generals.

The generals were not only the supreme military *Powers of the generals.* officers, but they had powers which raised them almost to the level of a cabinet or ministry of the present day. As military officers they had command over all the forces of the state, both military and naval. They provided for the safety of the land, the protection of the coasts, and the food supply of the town. They conducted the levy and raised funds for war purposes. They appointed the trierarchs. As the chief executive magistrates they had the right to summon the assembly, usually through the me-dium of the prytanes ; they were expected to pro-tect the state against treason and to maintain the democratic constitution. They had also the conduct of foreign affairs, and represented the state in its relations with other communities, arranging for the

---

[1] The Hellenotamiae were probably elected (Gilbert, **Handbuch,** i. p. 236). Sophocles was a member of this board (Hicks, Manual of Inscriptions, 30), and the younger Pericles (Dittenberger, Sylloge, 44).

2—2

conclusion of treaties and the fulfilment of obligations
so incurred[1].

The important powers exercised by the board of
generals gave it the position of the executive government, so long as it retained the confidence of the
assembly. On this account prominent politicians
strove to obtain a seat on the board, and we shall
see below that the elections of generals were events
of great political importance.

Theory that one general was commander-in-chief. There is good reason to believe that the generals
were not all equal in authority, that there were dif-
ferences of rank within the board, and that one man
in particular had a superiority both of dignity and
of power to the rest. This theory has only been
formulated within the last few years and is still
disputed[2]; it is so important for the right compre-
hension of the Athenian constitution and history
that it is worth while to summarize the evidence
for it.

The theory is that all generals were not, as has
hitherto been thought, of equal rank, sharing the
duties of chief command by alternation or by lot,
but that one general was the president of the board
for the year—πρύτανις τῶν στρατηγῶν—and had
powers greater than those of his colleagues. Again
on every expedition, on which a number of generals
went, one of them was always entrusted with the

[1] The above summary is taken mainly from Gilbert's Handbuch, i. pp. 222—4.

[2] Oncken, Athen und Hellas, ii. p. 46, vaguely recognized the
existence of such a commander-in-chief; Droysen, Hermes, ix. pp.
9—16, first stated the theory explicitly; Beloch, Att. Pol., Anhang
i. pp. 280—8, discusses it at length and gives the evidence.

chief command, the president himself naturally assuming this position, whenever he went on active service.

There is scarcely sufficient evidence to enable us to decide confidently either for or against the theory[1], but the balance of probability seems strongly in its favour. We know that in the Persian wars a single general was elected to take supreme command of the Athenian forces[2]; and the appointment of a commander-in-chief is also attested for the latter part of the fourth century[3]. There is nothing to disprove the existence of a similar institution for the intervening period. On the contrary, the efficient conduct of the Peloponnesian war and the obstinate resistance on the part of Athens point to a strongly organized military system[4], which could not possibly have existed had military operations been entrusted to a board of generals with absolutely equal powers.

Arguments in favour of the theory.

[1] One or two phrases in Plutarch point to differences of rank. Thus in Per. 13, Menippus is mentioned as ὑποστρατηγῶν to Pericles; and in Nic. 12, Nicias is chosen general πρῶτος for the Sicilian expedition, on which he seems to have had a superiority of rank; on the other hand the only statement which conflicts with this is the mention by Diodorus (xiii. 97, 106) of the command alternating day by day. This however is only an incidental reference, is quite unsupported by other authorities and is improbable in itself. Diodorus is probably transferring to this date the institutions of the 6th century, (Hdt. vi. 109.)

[2] This magistrate is called ὁ Ἀθηναίων στρατηγὸς in Herodotus; Themistocles, Aristides and Xanthippus all held this post (Hdt. viii. 4, 131, ix. 28). See Gilbert, Beiträge, p. 65, and Busolt, Griechische Geschichte, ii. p. 334.

[3] He was then called ὁ στρατηγὸς ὁ ἐπὶ τὰ ὅπλα, see Gilbert, Handbuch, i. p. 222.

[4] Droysen, ib. p. 15.

Assuming then that there were differences of rank
we have literary authority for them in the phrase ὁ
δεῖνα καὶ ξυνάρχοντες which frequently occurs in
inscriptions[1] and for which Thucydides' expression
ὁ δεῖνα δεύτερος, τρίτος...δέκατος αὐτός[2] is evidently the equivalent. There must be some reason
why one man is singled out by name, while the
others are simply mentioned as his colleagues; the
prominence thus given probably denoted a superiority of rank. Where the phrases are used with
reference to single expeditions, on which three or
four generals are employed, the officer named is not
necessarily the president of the board[3]; but where
all generals are obviously included, the reference
must be to the πρύτανις[4]. The appointment of such
a president would have been quite consistent with
the symmetry of Athenian institutions, as nearly all
magistrates formed boards of ten, of which one
member was usually president[5]. Perhaps these argu-

---

[1] C. I. A. i. 273 (Dittenberger 29) Ἱπποκράτης Χολαργεὺς καὶ
ξυνάρχοντες. The same phrase is used in the same inscription of
the ταμίαι τῆς θεοῦ, of the ταμίαι τῶν ἄλλων θεῶν and of the
Ἑλληνοταμίαι. Cf. also C.I.A. i. 180—3 (Dittenberger 36), C.I.A.
i. 188 (Dittenberger 44).

[2] Cf. Thuc. i. 61 and 62, where Καλλίας πέμπτος αὐτὸς is
repeated as Καλλίας...καὶ οἱ ξυνάρχοντες. It is used also of am-
bassadors, Thuc. v. 4, Xen. Hell. ii. 2. 17.

[3] In Thuc. ii. 79, iii. 3, iii. 19, the general evidently commanded
the expedition, but certainly was not πρύτανις. It is noteworthy
that when the commander-in-chief of an expedition died he was
not succeeded by one of his colleagues on the expedition, but
another general was sent from home to take his place; see Thuc.
i. 63—4.

[4] Thuc. i. 116, ii. 13, Περικλῆς δέκατος αὐτός.

[5] The evidence for such a presidency is in most cases the use

ments would not be enough to establish the custom. There is evidence of a more direct nature in the fact that again and again in our authorities we find single generals spoken of as exercising the most important powers individually, without reference to their colleagues[1]; while in many cases only one general is mentioned where evidently many or all were employed[2]. The general exercising these powers must have been at least *de facto* president, and the other

of the phrase ὁ δεῖνα καὶ ξυνάρχοντες, which is applied to many boards of magistrates. Thus Gilbert (Handbuch, i. p. 234) assumes the existence of such a president for the ταμίαι τῆς θεοῦ solely from the use of this phrase, although he refuses to draw a similar inference in the case of the generals. Hauvette-Besnault (Les stratèges athéniens, p. 52), who argues that there was no regular commander-in-chief, says "The title ὁ δεῖνα καὶ ξυνάρχοντες was usually applied to the president of a board of magistrates, but does not imply anything as to the duration of the office. It was employed to denote the annual chief of the ταμίαι τῶν ἱερῶν χρημάτων; it is no less often applied to the presidents of the Hellenotamiae, who constantly change." The change of presidents within this latter board is established by C. I. A. i. 188, in which five different names occur followed by the words καὶ ξυνάρχοντες. The reason however for the change of presidents on a board entrusted with the control of the revenue of the state is obvious; and the fact that we do not find a change of presidents similarly attested in the case of the generals, is negative evidence that one man held that position for a year.

[1] Thus Pericles seems to have been entrusted with full powers on more than one occasion (Thuc. ii. 22, 55). Similarly the conduct of Nicias in connection with the command at Pylos can only be explained on the theory that he was in supreme control of military affairs (Thuc. iv. 27, 42). See Droysen and Beloch, l. c.

[2] In Thuc. ii. 31 the Athenians go out πανδημεί Περικλέους στρατηγοῦντος; the other generals must have gone too. In v. 52 Alcibiades leads a large force to the Peloponnesus, but he was probably not the only general.

evidence will be enough perhaps to prove that he was also so *de jure*[1].

Import-ance of this position. If, then, we may assume the existence of such a president, he must have been the most important man in the state. In dignity he was formally raised above all other citizens, he was practically "President of the Republic." In power he was the head of the most important board of magistrates, and if we may compare this board to a modern cabinet, we may look upon him as a prime minister. The preeminence of this position made it the highest prize in the state, and it had great influence on politics.

The position of Athens as a power in Greece. There is one other subject which cannot be passed over, the position of Athens as a power in Greece. To discuss the division of parties we must know the subjects on which they were divided, and as during the period of the Peloponnesian war very few questions of home policy arose, and foreign affairs were all-important, it is necessary to understand the relation in which Athens stood to the other powers of Greece, in order to realize the attitude of parties to the different questions of foreign policy.

Athens and Sparta divided between them the Empire of Greece. Athens was preeminently a sea power. She was the mistress and leader of the sea states, as Sparta was of the land powers. Any pretensions she had to land empire she renounced in 445, and by this concession she obtained the recog-

---

[1] Gilbert (Beiträge, pp. 38, ff.) rejects the theory of a πρύτανις: he believes that in all cases where generals have superior authority they had been appointed αὐτοκράτορες. It is unreasonable to suppose that this extraordinary power was conferred so often. See Beloch, Att. Pol. pp. 285—6.

nition of her dominion of the sea. Here she was absolute: the sea was regarded as part of her territory, and as late as 419 it was regarded as a violation of her right for ships of war to cross it without her consent[1]. At the beginning of the war all the sea states with few exceptions were her subjects or allies[2].

This alliance was the source of her power. The relation of Athens to the confederacy of Delos had passed from that of leadership to that of dominion[3]; the original allies had with few exceptions become subjects[4].

Athens and the confederacy of Delos.

This process was the inevitable result of circumstances. If the league was to continue at all, the strongest power was bound to come to the front and the weaker states to renounce their independence[5]. To maintain the efficiency of the league for its original purposes it was necessary to retain unwilling members, forbid retirement and punish revolt[6]. For the same

---

[1] Thuc. v. 56, the Argives complain to the Athenians, ὅτι, γεγραμμένον ἐν ταῖς σπονδαῖς διὰ τῆς ἑαυτῶν ἑκάστους μὴ ἐᾶν πολεμίους διέναι, ἐάσειαν κατὰ θάλασσαν παραπλεῦσαι. The Athenians regarded this action of the Lacedaemonians as a violation of their alliance. The toll levied by the Athenians in the Bosporus is another instance of the same claim on the part of Athens to the exclusive control of the sea.

[2] All the eastern colonies of Greece, either on the islands or on the coast at a distance from Central Greece (e.g. Macedonia, Thrace, and Asia Minor) were members of the alliance.

[3] The ἡγεμονία had without design on her part become an ἀρχή. See Grote, v. pp. 146—152, cf. Thuc. i. 97—99.

[4] The members of the confederacy originally ξύμμαχοι, were now ὑπήκοοι; Thucydides calls them δοῦλοι. See Gilbert, Handbuch, i. pp. 392 and 405, and Thuc. i. 98, iii. 10, vi. 76.

[5] See Müller-Strübing, Aristophanes, pp. 81—2.

[6] Grote, v. 154. "The confederacy was perpetual and peremptory, not allowing retirement or evasion."

reason it was a matter of military expediency to strengthen the weak spots in the frontier of the league, to fill up the gaps, and to constrain independent and neutral states to join against their will, that they might not offer a place of vantage to the foe. The want of one link might weaken or destroy the whole chain. It was a question of self-preservation[1]; and the Athenians were only carrying this theory to a logical conclusion in seeking to win Thera and Melos. This is the argument underlying the Melian debate, although the selfishness of the policy is there presented with an exaggeration of brutality, that probably surpassed the truth[2].

The relation of Athens to her subjects was based on the power of the stronger, and perhaps justified the title of τυραννίς, which was employed by both friends and enemies to describe it[3].

Control of Athens over the affairs of the allies. Athens alone controlled the policy and administered the affairs of the league. The members were subject to a direct tax, assessed by Athens, paid into her treasury, and administered by her officers. Athens also interfered to a considerable extent with the constitution of some of the states[4], watched over

---

[1] Thuc. vi. 83, πᾶσι δὲ ἀνεπίφθονον τὴν προσήκουσαν σωτηρίαν ἐκπορίζεσθαι. Cf. also vi. 85.

[2] Cf. v. 99, τὸ ἀναγκαῖον τῆς ἀρχῆς. v. 91 (Athens is acting ἐπ᾽ ὠφελίᾳ τῆς ἡμετέρας ἀρχῆς καὶ ἐπὶ σωτηρίᾳ). v. 97 (besides the extension of the empire, the Melians would give a sense of security διὰ τὸ καταστραφῆναι).

[3] Pericles, Thuc. ii. 63. Cleon, iii. 37. The Mytilenaeans, iii. 10.

[4] Such interference chiefly took place after revolt, when the guilty oligarchy naturally gave place to a democracy. But there was no complete uniformity of constitution, and oligarchies were tolerated in the independent states (Lesbos and Chios), and

their civil administration by means of ἐπίσκοποι[1], occasionally put garrisons in under φρούραρχοι[2], and required all lawsuits of importance to be settled in the Athenian courts.

The subjection of the allies put Athenian power on an artificial basis, for it was opposed to the Grecian ideal of autonomy for each single state[3]. This violation of Greek national feeling, combined with the practical hardships of tribute and compulsory jurisdiction, naturally created enemies for Athens in the subject states ; but it will appear from a consideration of the circumstances that the discontented were a comparatively small body, and that the bulk of the allies were sincerely attached to the Athenian alliance.

The tribute was chiefly irksome from the method *Tribute.* in which it was raised and administered ; a common fund was a necessity, and the allies purchased by their contributions immunity from service which was undertaken by Athens. The amount of these contributions was never excessive, but the burden of it bore most heavily on the rich men[4] and they alone were offended.

possibly in some of the subject states (Samos, according to Grote's theory, vii. p. 218, n. 2).

[1] These were extraordinary officers, see Wilamowitz, Aus Kydathen, p. 16 and p. 75.

[2] Wilamowitz, ib. p. 73.

[3] It was with a view to this feeling that Sparta professed to undertake τὴν ἐλευθέρωσιν τῆς Ἑλλάδος. The enslavement of the Athenian allies and the possible subjection of the rest of Greece are prominently brought forward by the enemies of Athens. Cf. Thuc. i. 68, 122.

[4] It is probable that in most states it was assessed on a graduated scale like the Athenian εἰσφορά.

Compulsory jurisdiction.
Of the grievance caused by the compulsory jurisdiction of Athens we hear much more both from ancient and modern writers[1]. It is usually regarded as a piece of unqualified despotism, due in part to the desire of Athens to interfere with the allies in peace as well as in war, in part to the litigious instincts of the Athenian people[2]. In reality, as Grote points out, it arose from the necessity (which is common to all political unions) of having some judicial authority to decide disputes within the league.

When different states combine there must be some tribunal to which differences may be referred, which would otherwise result in war. Consequently we see a provision for this purpose inserted in most treaties[3]. So in the Delian confederacy the disputes between two members of the league, at first referred to the common synod at Delos, were brought to an Athenian court: this practice gradually became extended to disputes between individuals of

---

[1] In this argument I am following Oncken, Athen und Hellas, ii. pp. 110—127, who has worked out Grote's theory with great ability.

[2] Thuc. i. 77. Resp. Ath. i. 16.

[3] Cf. Thuc. i. 77 (the Athenian jurisdiction took the place of violence in other empires, without inflicting injustice). Arbitration within leagues was always regarded as of great importance, and, as to-day, as a substitute for war. It was the refusal of Samos to submit to arbitration which led to the Samian war, Plut. Per. 25. So Corcyra offers to submit to arbitration, Thuc. i. 28. Cf. v. 27 (in the Argive-Corinthian alliance any state may enter ἥτις αὐτόνομός τέ ἐστι καὶ δίκας ἴσας καὶ ὁμοίας δίδωσι). Arrangements for submitting possible disputes to arbitration are almost the only subject of the Argive and Lacedaemonian alliance, Thuc. v. 77.

different states, finally to the more serious disputes between members of the same state[1].

It seems highly probable that the purpose underlying this was the prevention of political conflicts and civil war. It was in the interests of the league generally that the members should not be weakened by στάσις, and that one political party should not be able to oppress the other, and then abuse the protection of the law to punish its opponents.

It was expedient that there should be some authority, standing above the disputants, to decide between them: and this they had in the Athenian courts. We may assume that the greater number of the charges brought to Athens for trial were for political offences[2]; and as the oligarchs were usually ill-disposed to Athens, that the trials were for conspiring against the democracy.

The oligarchs in this respect also can alone have felt injured by the system. We may therefore conclude that the jurisdiction of Athens over the cities of the league was beneficial to the greater number

[1] That this was the result of a gradual process is proved by the fact that there were no universal regulations compelling disputes between citizens of the allied states to be tried at Athens. The constraint depended on no general principles but on separate treaties in each case. See Fränkel, n. 641 to Böckh.

[2] This is supported by a number of passages in the Resp. Ath. which can only refer to trials for political offences. i. 16, τοὺς μὲν τοῦ δήμου σώζουσι, τοὺς δ' ἐναντίους ἀπολλύουσιν ἐν τοῖς δικαστηρίοις κ.τ.λ. Cf. i. 14. Cf. also Aristophanes, quoted below p. 66, n. 1. That there was ground for these charges is proved sufficiently by the fact that the oligarchs were always the moving force in revolt from Athens: and that it was a matter of political principle with them to work against and overthrow the democracy.

of the allies.   Not only was there a settled state of
peace within the league, but there was a security of
person and property, and a protection for the people
against the oppression of the rich oligarchs and
against the injustice of Athenian officers.

Attach-
ment of
democrats
to the
Athenian
alliance.

The democracies in the different states had good
reason to be attached to the alliance, and they were
probably actuated by a warmer feeling than that of
indifferent acquiescence, which Grote thought characteristic of them[1]. There was a community of interest,
a solidarity of democratic feeling which supported
the confederacy. 'The Athenian empire is in its
essence the alliance of Hellenic democrats against
the internal enemy—the oligarchy—which is always
conspiring or ready to conspire with the barbarians[2].'

From this point of view the confederacy was in
the main as much a voluntary league in the time of
the Peloponnesian war, as in the days of Aristides.
From the fundamental principle of democracy (the
government in most of the states), if the people
wished to have what they regarded as the benefits
of Athenian government—protection from external
and internal foes—at the cost of tribute, the alliance was of mutual advantage[3]. The Athenians
found in it a chief cause of their strength, the
allies found protection and enjoyed security of com-

---

[1] Thuc. iii. 47, νῦν μὲν γὰρ ὑμῖν ὁ δῆμος ἐν πάσαις ταῖς πόλεσιν
εὔνους ἐστίν. This is emphatic testimony. Cf. also viii. 48, τὸν δὲ
δῆμον σφῶν (allies) τε καταφυγὴν εἶναι καὶ ἐκείνων (oligarchs) σωφρο-
νιστήν.

[2] Oncken, Athen und Hellas, ii. p. 116.

[3] Isocr. Paneg. 103 ff. lays stress on the benefits of the Athenian
Empire.

merce and maritime traffic, as well as peace and
order at home.

It was otherwise with the oligarchic minority. *Discontent of the oligarchs.* They had reason to hate the dominion of Athens. It was they who bore the burden of the tribute, and who were liable to prosecution at Athens: and in addition to these two grievances, they felt the discontent common to the oligarchs in all Greek states, because they were deprived of the privileges and powers of government, to which on their principles their wealth and birth entitled them. On this account they were ready to combine with the enemies of Athens and to break from their allegiance; and just as there was a solidarity of democracies throughout Greece, so there was a network of oligarchic combination between the different states—an "*Adelskette*"—embracing Athens and most of the allies, always ready, if opportunities were favourable, to combine with Sparta, and to overthrow the democratic government[1].

There was, indeed, an inseparable connection between oligarchy and disloyalty to Athens on the part of the allies. As soon as the allies broke from Athens, the oligarchs got the upper hand[2], so that

[1] Cf. Müller-Strübing, Aristophanes, pp. 83—84. "Sparta was the proper centre of reaction against Athenian dominion, but even in Athens there was a link of the 'Adelskette.'" In Thuc. viii. 48 Phrynichus says that the oligarchs had promised the allies oligarchical constitutions in the event of the Athenian empire being overthrown. This must refer to previous communications between oligarchs in Athens and the allied states.

[2] The oligarchs were always responsible for the revolt, and Sparta supported them against the democracy. Thus, after the

revolt was the first step in establishing their influence; and conversely as soon as the oligarchs got
power, the alliance was broken off[1].

*Connec-
tion be-
tween the
demo-
cracy, the
alliance
and the
war.*

Democracy was, therefore, the bond of union between Athens and her allies: while oligarchy was
almost synonymous with revolt. On this account
the continuance of the alliance depended on the
maintenance of the Athenian democracy. The alliance and the democracy were mutually indispen-
sable. For while the alliance would be shattered by
oligarchy, the democracy of Athens was supported
by the alliance, which was the main source of her
strength[2]. Many of the allies served in the armies
and on the fleet of Athens, and in addition to the
tribute contributed in this way to her power. Moreover the empire of the sea ensured Athens complete
control of trade[3], which was of vital importance to
her as a commercial community.

In the same way the war was equally necessary

general revolt which began in 412 we hear that Lysander used his
influence in favour of the oligarchs. Plut. Lys. 5.

[1] In the earlier part of the war the movement for revolt is
always initiated by the oligarchs. The case of Lesbos was typical;
Thuc. iii. 47 (Diodotus says the people do not join *the oligarchs in
revolt*, implying that the latter were always to blame). Cf. Resp.
Ath. i. 14 (if οἱ πλούσιοι καὶ οἱ ἰσχυροί rule in the cities, ὀλίγιστον
χρόνον ἡ ἀρχὴ ἔσται τοῦ δήμου τοῦ Ἀθήνῃσι). This is supported by
Thuc. viii. 64, (he describes Thasos as revolting as soon as
oligarchy was established, δοκεῖν δέ μοι καὶ ἐν ἄλλοις πολλοῖς τῶν
ὑπηκόων). Chios forms an exception to this, as it remained faithful till 412, even under an oligarchy; but the revolt then proceeded
from the oligarchs.

[2] Thuc. i. 143, τὰ τῶν ξυμμάχων ὅθεν ἰσχύομεν. iii. 13, δι' ἥν ἡ
Ἀττικὴ ὠφελεῖται. iii. 46, ἰσχύομεν δὲ πρὸς τοὺς πολεμίους τῷδε.

[3] Böckh, i. p. 69.

to maintain the alliance. The war was forced on Athens by Sparta with a view to break up the alliance, and the main cause of it was the jealousy felt by Sparta for the growing power of Athens[1]. Other causes naturally contributed to it, and chief among these the antithesis between democracy and oligarchy, which had divided the states of Greece from the time that Athens first formed a counter alliance to Sparta[2]. Hence the war became in course of time a conflict of political principles; community of feeling and interest joined democrats on the one side against oligarchs on the other; advantage was taken of internal differences[3], and the area of the war became extended as states hitherto neutral entered on it in support of those with whom they were politically in sympathy. Consequently, as in the case of the Athenian confederacy, a change of constitution carried with it a change of side, and a change of side was usually accompanied by the overthrow of the existing constitution. This is well illustrated by the conduct of Argos, who joined the Athenian alliance, as a democratic state[4], but with the rise of oligarchic feeling went over to Sparta, and soon established an oligarchy[5]. This government

[1] Thucydides is careful to insist on every possible occasion that the *real* (as opposed to the pretended) cause of the war was Sparta's fear of the growth of the Athenian empire. See Thuc. i. 23, 33, 86, 88, 118, 140.

[2] Cf. Isocr. Paneg. 16. Thuc. iii. 82.

[3] Cf. the attack on Plataea, Thuc. ii. 2; on Boeotia, Thuc. iv. 76. See Vischer, Kleine Schriften, i. p. 78.

[4] They regarded Athens as πόλιν τε σφίσι φιλίαν ἀπὸ παλαιοῦ καὶ δημοκρατουμένην ὥσπερ καὶ αὐτοί, Thuc. v. 44.

[5] Thuc. v. 76, (the motives of the oligarchs were to obtain

was overthrown by a democratic reaction and the alliance with Athens was restored.

The Peloponnesian war a conflict between democracy and oligarchy. The war was therefore not only a trial of strength between the two great powers of Greece, it was a life and death struggle between the principles of oligarchic and democratic government[1]. The danger threatened even the constitution of Athens as well as her empire; for there were many of her citizens who would gladly have seen oligarchy established at the price of submission to Sparta.

These men as soon as they attained power began to treat with Sparta[2]: and there was some ground for the democratic feeling that peace with Sparta, except on terms which would be a compensation for the past and a guarantee for the future, was likely to lead to the rise of philo-Spartan influence, and bring the danger to democracy all the nearer.

Principles of democratic policy. I have argued that the democratic constitution and the war were both necessary to maintain the alliance; and that to a certain degree the continuance of the war to a decisive end was demanded in the interests of the democracy. These are the cardinal principles of democratic policy, and we shall not wonder that without flinching the democratic party maintained them for twenty-seven years.

alliance with Sparta, καὶ οὕτως ἤδη τῷ δήμῳ ἐπιτίθεσθαι); cf. c. 81.

[1] This is true in the main throughout the war; it was fully proved at the end of the war, when Lysander established oligarchies in every town.

[2] In 411. The peace made in 404 was largely due to oligarchic intrigue and was followed by an overthrow of the democracy.

CHAPTER II.

DIVISION AND COMPOSITION OF PARTIES.

THE antithesis between democracy and oligarchy, *Democracy and oligarchy as principles of party division.* which ranged all the states of Greece in different camps, appeared also within these states, and was one of the most important causes of party division[1]. Hence in Athens, as elsewhere, we find men of certain political sympathies described as oligarchs and as democrats: and the reality of these distinctions is established not only by the general agreement of our authorities, but by the events of 411 and 405, when the two parties came to blows for their political principles.

But apart from the academic preference, which *Parties divided on questions of policy.* most men must have had for one form of constitution or the other, these principles do not form a satisfactory ground for the classification of parties. The difference between the champions of the two extreme forms of government admitted of no compromise; the dispute, when once raised, had to be fought out to the bitter end; and at Athens to advocate any

---

[1] Cf. Plut. Per. 11, ἦν μὲν γὰρ ἐξ ἀρχῆς διπλόη τις ὕπουλος, ὥσπερ ἐν σιδήρῳ, διαφορὰν ὑποσημαίνουσα δημοτικῆς καὶ ἀριστοκρατικῆς προαιρέσεως, ἡ δ' ἐκείνων ἅμιλλα καὶ φιλοτιμία τῶν ἀνδρῶν βαθυτάτην τομὴν τεμοῦσα τῆς πόλεως τὸ μὲν δῆμον τὸ δ' ὀλίγους ἐποίησε καλεῖσθαι.

proposal injurious to the democracy was an act of high treason. In cases like this, at least until issue is joined, men in pronounced antagonism to the existing constitution do not usually form a political party, but work in secret, seeking to gain advantage from the ordinary course of practical politics. So at Athens, except for the brief intervals of revolutionary movements, the oligarchs generally kept their projects in the background, and parties were divided not so much by fixed principles, as by the ordinary politics of the day and questions of administration[1]. Of these in the period under consideration the question of war and peace was by far the most important.

We may conclude, therefore, that as a cause of party division, the democratic policy had much more weight than the democratic constitution ; and in order to understand how political parties were ranged, we must find out who supported and who opposed a particular policy. If we consider the democratic policy during the war, we shall find that the oligarchs did not form the bulk of the opposition; many of them may have taken an active part in resisting it, while others of them held aloof from politics ; but the majority of the standing opposition was formed, so far as we can see, of men of moderate views, indifferent but not disloyal to the constitution.

A third political party.   If this conclusion is right, there is a third political party to be considered. Such a party scarcely receives explicit mention in our authorities[2], a fact which may

---

[1] Beloch, Att. Pol. pp. 1 and 13.

[2] In n. 1 p. 92 I have discussed the passages in which this party is referred to.

be attributed in part to the deficiencies which cha-
racterize them, in part to the vagueness of party
division: but its existence is, I think, satisfactorily
demonstrated by the history of political events.

If we look to the early history of Athens, the *Rise of*
rise of this party can be traced. From the begin- *this party.*
nings of political conflict in Athens, there had always been a considerable party in opposition to the
democrats and their policy; and every step in the
progress of reform was opposed more or less vehe-
mently by the aristocrats, though the force of events
and in particular the commercial development of
Athens had ensured the triumph of the democrats
on every occasion.

From the year 460 the aristocrats had no more
privileges to defend against the advance of democracy, and could only carry their principles into effect
by reaction[1]. The political victory of Pericles over
Cimon broke the force of the aristocracy for a time,
but Thucydides, the son of Melesias, united the
opposition in a strong party[2], and the struggle was
renewed. In the resort to ostracism in 444 Thucydides was defeated, and the old aristocratic party
was dissolved[3].

Henceforth politics were transformed; for the

---

[1] Cf. Plut. Cim. 15, (Cimon wished to restore the "aristocratic" government of Clisthenes).

[2] Plut. Per. 11. Müller-Strübing, Aristophanes, pp. 295—7,
thinks that this party was largely composed of the peasants, as
Thucydides would not have challenged ostracism without strength
of numbers, and that we have here the frequent opposition between
town and country.

[3] Plut. Per. 14.

time Pericles was supreme and above all parties,
and during his life the opposition was hopelessly dis-
organized. After his death, when political struggles
were renewed, and party divisions again became prominent, we find the opposition to the democratic
policy organized under the leadership of Nicias.
The history of the succeeding years shows us a large
body of men, combined under recognized leaders
and following a consistent policy.

This body may on these grounds be fairly regarded as a political party in opposition to the democrats. Its members were, however, quite distinct from
the oligarchs; they were not hostile to the constitution,
and though they may have criticized its defects, they
were not eager to change it; they were men of
moderate views opposed to the democratic policy.

*Three poli-
tical
parties.*
We can therefore distinguish three political parties, the two extremes of oligarchy and democracy
and the intermediate section, corresponding to the
modern divisions of right, left and centre. These
political sections were not sharply divided; parties
were more or less in solution and had a tendency to
merge in one another. The oligarchs, especially, as
they could not declare their aims, but pursued them
secretly, attached themselves to whatever policy they
thought would best advance them, and only on rare
occasions organized themselves for a decisive effort.
With these qualifications we may distinguish the
three parties[1] as (1) The democrats proper, or the
democrats from conviction, shading off into (2) the

---

[1] I am indebted to Dr Beloch (Att. Pol. p. 13) for the titles
" democrats from conviction," and " opportunist democrats."

middle party, mainly composed of moderate or opportunist democrats, but including also some moderate
oligarchs, who serve as a link to (3) the oligarchs
proper, opposed by conviction to democracy and
eager to overthrow it, but not as a party taking a
prominent part in ordinary political life.

Having settled the main lines of party division, *Composi-*
the subject, which naturally suggests itself for discus- *tion of parties.*
sion, is the composition of the different parties, or
the relation in which they stand to the different
sections of the population considered from the point
of view of wealth and occupation.

I have argued that as a cause of division questions of the day were of more importance than the
permanent principles men entertained on the subject
of the constitution.   On this account we must determine what policy was in accordance with the interests of the different classes, before we can understand
how the parties were composed.   Generally speaking
a man's political position is mainly determined by
his class interests, and in the case of Athens the
importance of economic considerations has been generally recognized.   Thus Böckh[1] says, "the great war
between aristocracy and democracy always going on
in Greece was largely a war of possessors and non-
possessors," while other writers[2] regard the conflict of
parties as nothing else than a war of rich against poor.

---

[1] Böckh, i. p. 182. This too is Plato's description, (Rep. iv. 422
E). "Each city is composed of at least two cities, hostile to each
other—rich and poor."

[2] This is the main argument of W. L. Freese in his book "Der
Parteikampf der Reichen und der Armen in Athen"; cf. Beloch,
Att. Pol., pp. 1, 2.

*Popula-
tion of
Attica.*
In order to understand and apply this conclusion it is necessary to have a clear view of the population of Attica in its economic aspect.

The total population at the beginning of the war may be regarded, at the most probable estimate, as about 250,000[1], made up as follows:—35,000 citizens of full age, representing a total citizen population of about 105,000; 10,000 metoecs, who with their families amounted to about 30,000, and about 100,000 slaves.

*Agricultu-
ral class a
majority.*
Of the Athenian citizens at the beginning of the war the greater number lived in the country cultivating their own farms. This fact we have on the explicit statement of Thucydides[2], and there seems no reason to reject his statement, as we know that the land of Attica was very much divided. Notwithstanding the war, which must have had a disastrous effect on population and property, we are told that even in 403 out of a probable total of 20,000 citizens there were only 5000 who owned no land[3].

Of these landowners all did not live on their

[1] This is the estimate of Beloch, Bevölkerung, p. 73, and is in sharp conflict with that of Böckh, which is double this number (i. p. 51). For a discussion of the grounds on which the former is based I would refer to Dr Beloch's work. To me his arguments appear conclusive.

[2] ii. 14 and 16.

[3] Dionysius in the argument to Lysias 23. It is somewhat difficult to believe that three-fourths of the population were even then possessed of landed property. Müller-Strübing (Philologus, Supplementband, iv. p. 62) thinks that the 5000 represented more than half the citizens, but the total of 20,000 has been accepted by Böckh, Büchsenschütz and Freese, as well as by Beloch in his examination of the population of Attica, ib. p. 99.

estates; many of the richer men especially resided in
the town, either leasing their property or having it
worked by slaves[1].

From these considerations we may conclude that
in spite of the commercial changes fostered by
Themistocles and Pericles the class interested in
agriculture must have formed a majority of the
population.

Of the rest of the citizens many of the richer men
either were engaged personally in industry and commerce or at least profited by them, in lending their
capital at a high rate of interest; but the bulk of the
inhabitants of the town and the Piraeus must have
been poor men, as much reduced to the necessity of
manual labour[2] as the poor aliens and slaves, who
with them formed the industrial class.

Such was the division of classes according to
occupation; on the distribution of wealth we have
not such definite information. At the beginning of
the war there were about 15 to 16,000 Athenians
of at least hoplite census, as opposed to 19 to
20,000 Thetes[3]. The classes owning a substantial
property formed therefore almost half the citizens;
but the Thetes must not all be considered as
poor men. Many owned small plots of land, which
raised them above our standard of poverty[4], and

*Distribu-
tion of
wealth.*

---

[1] Böckh, i. p. 53.

[2] Ib., i. p. 58; cf. Plato, Rep. viii. 565 A.

[3] Beloch, ib. p. 70. In the use of the term Thetes, I have
assumed that all property was taken into account in arranging the
classes for the εἰσφορά; Böckh, i. 189, argues that in the time of
the Peloponnesian war other property than land was so included.

[4] Thus Freese, ib. p. 28, points out that Antipater and Cassander

Böckh's[1] estimate of the national wealth (which he puts roughly at 1 talent on the average to each citizen) points to a general state of well-being. We may assume that a large majority of citizens were either possessed of a fair amount of property, or were in a position to earn their living without trouble.

Theory that many Athenians lived on state pay. In connection with this subject I cannot pass by a theory of which we hear so much from some historians, that Athens supported by means of pay for state services a large mob of professional idlers. We have just seen that this mob could only have been composed of those inhabitants of Athens and the Piraeus, who had neither land nor capital to support them, and who, presumably, preferred the meagre contributions from the state to the wages they might earn by honest labour[2]. The ordinary rate of industrial wages (as of interest) was high in

in excluding the poor from citizenship required a minimum of 10 or 20 minae, a sum which in the altered value of money and interest we should consider high.

[1] i. p. 146. Each talent would bear interest of 700 drachmae a year.

[2] This is the central idea of Freese's book. He argues (pp. 35—41), in opposition to Böckh, that the number of citizens engaged in manual labour was utterly inconsiderable, and that almost the whole of the work was done by metoecs and slaves. It is, of course, impossible to say what proportion of poor Athenians had a trade or handicraft; but even accepting his own statement of the distribution of landed property, there can scarcely have been more than a fourth of the population, to whom state pay offered any attraction, so that the institution cannot have had the far reaching effect, which he attributes to it. The question, whether the wages for state services were sufficient to compete with the rewards of industry can be more easily discussed, and the conclusion is equally unfavourable to Freese's theory.

Athens, in spite of the competition of metoec and slave[1]. On the other hand, the ordinary wages for those state services with which we are chiefly concerned were low and in great part precarious. The wages in question are those for the army and fleet, those for the council of the Five Hundred and those for the law courts[2].

The wages for the army scarcely concern the argument. *Pay of the army.* Obviously an idle city rabble could not depend on military wages in time of peace, and even in war the men usually enrolled as hoplites belonged to the higher classes, and the Thetes were only exceptionally employed. Again, the wages both for army and fleet were not so high as those that could be got in industrial production. Service on the fleet, moreover, was the concern of metoecs and foreigners rather than of citizens. The latter manned the two state galleys, and served as marines, but the rowers were, at least in the period under discussion, mainly either metoecs or foreigners[3].

---

[1] Böckh, i. p. 148, says "from the extreme cheapness of the necessaries of life, the wages of labour must have been lower than to-day: the number of competitors in the market for labour, Thetes, metoecs and slaves must have produced a greater diminution." But Fränkel, n. 202 to Böckh, l.c. (on the authority of inscriptions recently discovered) puts wages as high as $1\frac{1}{2}$ and $2\frac{1}{2}$ drachmae a day; and the fact that metoecs were attracted to Athens points to wages being higher there than elsewhere, while slaves were simply a commercial investment, so that competition would not be carried beyond the limit of a satisfactory return.

[2] The argument that many people lived on state pay loses much of its force in the light of later investigation, which has shown that *pay for the assembly* did not exist before Euclides. (Fränkel, n. 427 to Böckh.)

[3] The proportion of marines to rowers was about 10 to 190.

Pay of the council. The council consisted of 500 men, and as its duties absorbed the whole of their time, they received a wage of one drachma a day. As this, like the pay for the army, was in return for definite services, it was not likely to encourage idleness, while as only five hundred men were concerned, the bulk of the poorer citizens could not have been interested in it.

Pay of the dicasts. There remains for consideration the pay of the dicasts. Leaving out of view the number of dicasts usually employed, and the number of days in the year on which they were likely to receive pay[1], the amount at which it was fixed made it only a contribution to the expenses of life[2], and it certainly was not enough to relieve the recipient from all necessity to labour. Though a better remuneration than the nominal jury fee of to-day, it can scarcely have been a temptation to perpetual idleness, and as a matter of fact the judges are usually represented as old men[3], whose working days are over.

The authorities on the composition of the fleet are quoted by Gilbert, Handbuch, i. p. 234, and Adolph Bauer in Müller's Handbuch Gr. Alt., p. 282. See Thuc. i. 121, Resp. Ath. i. 12.

[1] From Ar. Vesp. 360 it has been supposed that 6000 dicasts were chosen every year and all employed 300 days. Aristophanes, however, does not say this, and Fränkel (Die attischen Geschworenengerichte pp. 10—19) throws great doubt on the conclusion. He thinks that the number of dicasts employed was much smaller, and that there were not more than 240 days a year when judicial business was possible. The importance of the dicasts' pay to the democracy is discussed below, p. 70.

[2] Böckh, i. p. 152. The fee was usually 2 obols, raised temporarily from 425 to 3 obols to compensate for the rise of prices caused by the war.

[3] As the chorus in Ar. Vesp.; cf. Ach. 375, Eq. 255. Throughout the Vespae emphasis is laid on the small amount of the pay, see especially 702 ff.

To sum up, we may conclude that the theory of an idle city rabble living on state pay is a gross exaggeration, not supported by facts; that the number to whom the system could have offered any inducement was comparatively small[1], the number to whom regular employment other than military service was open was still smaller, and the pay offered could not have competed in attraction with the average wages of labour. State pay existed as a partial compensation to the ordinary citizen for his loss of time, not as a means of subsistence for the idle and improvident.

We may now return to consider the relation which classes bore to political parties. To repeat my former conclusions, the population may be divided into (1) a class of rich men living on their land, on the interest of their capital or by trade; (2) a large middle class, composed of men of hoplite census; and (3) the class of Thetes, comprising a certain number of farmers, safely removed from poverty, but ranking in this class, and a considerable industrial section without capital depending for subsistence on the produce of their labour.

To compare these with the political parties distinguished above, it is immediately obvious that there is a broad analogy between the rich and the oligarchs, the poor and the democrats, and the middle class and the middle party[2].

Connection between classes and political parties.

---

[1] The number of those who could not support themselves by labour must have increased in the latter part of the war, when agriculture was at a standstill, but at that time the population had seriously diminished and the army and fleet made constant and increasing demands.

[2] This analogy is borne out by the titles given to the different

This analogy corresponded approximately both to the actual state of the parties, and to their respective interests. Without going into details, which will have to be discussed in a closer examination of the different parties, the rich men had a natural inclination to an oligarchical form of government, in which privileges and power compensated them for the burdens they bore; the poorest classes realized the advantages of democracy, in which every man was equal and taxation was proportional to wealth, while the middle classes were not enthusiastic for either extreme.

Similarly it will be found that in the main the policy of the oligarchs favoured the rich, and that of the democrats the poor, while the middle party pursued the ends determined by their interests.

To this broad analogy there were of course many exceptions, as the circumstances or convictions of individuals separated them from the rest of their class; it is sufficient to point out now that the position of the average man was determined by the interests of the class to which he belonged.

parties (these are discussed in the next chapter). Thus the oligarchs are called δυνατοί and πλούσιοι, the democrats οἱ πολλοί and πένητες. The identity is assumed by Euripides (Supp. 238 ff.), where he speaks of three parties in the state, οἱ ὄλβιοι, οἱ οὐκ ἔχοντες, ἥ 'ν μέσῳ μοῖρα. In Aristotle the μέσοι are both the middle class and the middle party. Pol. 1295 b.

CHAPTER III.

§ 1. *The Democratic Party.*

THE first party to be considered is that of the *Titles of the different parties.* democrats proper, the 'democrats from conviction,' who are so called in contrast to the middle party, the members of which, though for the most part democrats, formed a separate party. Some information of the way in which the democrats were regarded by their contemporaries may be obtained from the titles applied to them. As these titles were usually invented and employed by writers in opposition to the democracy, the complimentary title was naturally chosen by the oligarchs, and the term of abuse applied to their opponents.

The first and most common title of the democrats is neutral; they are called ὁ δῆμος[1], i.e. *the* popular party, τὸ πλῆθος or οἱ πολλοί, the numbers of the democrats appearing great in proportion to those of the ὀλίγοι.

---

[1] These titles are so well known and occur so often that it is unnecessary to quote the evidence for their use. Freese, Parteikampf der Reichen und der Armen, pp. 24—5, gives most of them.

Secondly, the oligarchs are frequently called πλούσιοι, δυνατοί, and though the term is not used as a
party phrase Xenophon talks of ὁ δῆμος as οἱ πένητες
τῶν πολιτῶν[1].

A third class of names points to the contrast
with respect to birth and culture. The oligarchs
assumed the titles of καλοὶ κἀγαθοί, βέλτιστοι,
γνώριμοι, and above all of χρηστοί, while the democrats were styled πονηροί, μοχθηροὶ and the like[2].

---

[1] Xen. Mem. iv. 2, 37. Cf. Resp. Ath. i. 2, and Plut. Per. 7,
where πολλοὶ καὶ πένητες is opposed to ὀλίγοι καὶ πλούσιοι.

[2] The application of uncomplimentary terms to denote political
opponents has always been frequent. Such terms, at first employed in mere abuse, gradually obtain literary recognition and
come into use as ordinary party titles. There is some significance
in the words chosen to describe the Athenian democracy. The
opposition of χρηστοί and πονηροί occurs throughout the Respub-
lica Atheniensium; the author uses other words to describe parties
(e.g. δῆμος, πένητες, and δημοτικοὶ are contrasted with γενναῖοι and
πλούσιοι, i. 2), but none so frequently as πονηρὸς and its opposite.
The use of πονηρὸς in connection with the Athenian democracy is
very general: see especially Thuc. viii. 47 (where Alcibiades uses
πονηρία as synonymous with δημοκρατία), Ar. Eccl. 176 (where the
antithesis between χρηστὸς and πονηρὸς is brought out), and Eur.
Supp. 243 (in which the poet refers to πονηροὶ προστάται, a phrase
which ocurs also in Ar. l.c.). In Aristot. Pol. 1294 a, 2 πονηρο-
κρατεῖσθαι is contrasted with ἀριστοκρατεῖσθαι. The word μοχθηρὸς
is not so frequent in a political sense, but it is found in several
passages as a substitute for πονηρὸς with exactly the same meaning. Thus in Ar. Eq. 1303, Thuc. viii. 73, Plut. Arist. 7, Nic.
11, it is employed to describe Hyperbolus, while in the same
passages in Thuc. and Plut. Nic., in Plut. Alc. 13, and Ar. Pax 681
πονηρὸς is used of the same man. Similarly Xen. (Hell. i. 4. 13)
in describing the prosecution of Alcibiades in 415 talks of οἱ μοχ-
θηρότερα λέγοντες as having driven him out, an expression which
recalls Thuc. vi. 89 (where Alcibiades speaks of those οἱ ἐπὶ τὰ
πονηρότερα ἐξῆγον τὸν ὄχλον). Cf. also Ar. Lys. 576, and Ran. 421,
Aristot. Pol. 1320 a, 34 (μοχθηρὰ δημοκρατία). The choice of these

Separating from these titles the abusive associa- *Democra-*
tions connected with them, they point to the fact *tic party*
mainly
that the δῆμος was largely composed of the poorer *composed*
of poorer
classes, who were reduced to the necessity of manual *classes.*
labour in agriculture or trade, and who could not
afford the education and leisure considered essential
by the rich. This inference is supported by the conclusion arrived at in the last chapter that the democratic party found its chief support in the poorer
classes, although there were many of the middle
and richer classes, especially among the merchants
and manufacturers, who gave an enthusiastic allegiance to the democracy and its policy[1]; in fact
both the leading politicians and the leading generals were usually men of some degree of wealth
and often of birth, whose attachment to the democracy, though it depended in part on the power and
distinction conferred upon them[2], was mainly a
matter of conviction.

The peasant farmers of small property, whose
income ranked them with the poorer classes, must
have been sincerely devoted to the democratic con-

particular terms may possibly have had some connection with their
original meaning of *laborious* (cf. **Ar. Vesp.** 466 πόνῳ πονηρέ), and
the application of them may have arisen from the idea, common to
the philosophy of the age, that manual labour was degrading in
itself and fatal to a life of culture or political activity. **Cf.** Socrates in Aelian, Var. Hist. x. 14 (ἡ ἀργία ἀδελφὴ τῆς ἐλευθερίας),
Aristot. Pol. 1269 a, 34 (on the necessity of σχολὴ in a well-ordered
state), and ib. 1278 a, 8 (the best constitution excludes the βάναυ-
σος from citizenship).

[1] Lysicles, Eucrates, Cleon, and Hyperbolus all came from the
trading class.

[2] This is the motive attributed to them by Thuc. viii. 73.

stitution, for any other would have excluded them from political privileges, but in their attitude to the war they must at first have been at one with the rest of the agricultural class. These men, therefore, while sincerely attached to the democracy, cannot always have regarded the democratic policy with favour, and probably formed a floating element, changing with the course of events from the middle party to the democrats, until by the loss of their property and their adaptation to new circumstances they became identified with the demos of the town.

Strength of the democratic party.   The constant supporters of the democratic policy, so far as we can judge from the course of events[1], formed almost half the citizen body. Consequently the accession of a comparatively few men from the less decided political sections sufficed to give to this party an effective voice in the assembly. On matters of administration and of less political interest the democrats could often command a chance majority, inasmuch as the greater part of their supporters dwelt in the town and the Piraeus, while the other parties were more scattered, and were not so careful in attending the assembly.

Organiza- tion of the democratic party.   For both these reasons it was necessary for this party to be well organized under recognized leaders. Organization was comparatively easy; they were for the most part men of similar sympa- thies and aims, and they alone of all parties were firmly united in the pursuit of a consistent policy.

---

[1] I have discussed in the next chapter the struggle of parties, and have endeavoured to show that for a time at least they were almost equally divided.

Besides organization they needed men to represent
their interests and give voice to their policy. The
demagogues were the party agents of the democracy. Of these one had a special preeminence and
so appears more frequently in our authorities. This
was the προστάτης τοῦ δήμου[1].

• At one time it was thought that this title de- *The προστάτης τοῦ δήμου.*
noted a magistrate with definite powers, but Arnold
and Grote have shown that it is purely unofficial, and
was only used to describe the leading demagogue,
who acted as guardian and representative of the
demos, as the ordinary προστάτης did of the metoec.
It was equivalent to δημαγωγός[2] with a notion of
primacy. His power was entirely dependent on the
support of the assembly[3], but his position compared
with that of other speakers was recognized as special
and preeminent[4].

We may therefore follow Grote in his denial that *Grote's theory wrong.*
the προστασία conferred any official power or respon-

[1] This phrase or its equivalent occurs often, especially in
connection with Athenian politics. Thuc. ii. 65 (Pericles' successors quarrelled περὶ τῆς τοῦ δήμου προστασίας). vi. 89 (Alcibiades
speaks of ἡ προστασία τοῦ δήμου). viii. 65 (of Androcles). viii.
89 (of the oligarchic leaders bidding for popular favour). Ar. Eq.
1128 (Demos says he likes to keep ἕνα προστάτην); cf. Pax 681,
Ran. 569, Eccl. 176, and Lys. 13. 7.

[2] In Thuc. iv. 21 Cleon is called δημαγωγός; cf. Ar. Eq. 191,
where ἡ δημαγωγία is evidently equivalent to ἡ προστασία.

[3] See Grote, vii. p. 303, also Gilbert, Beiträge, p. 78.

[4] Cf. the passages quoted in n. 1, which show that the position was regarded as definite and open to competition. Cf. also
Ar. Eq. 128—30, where in discussing the succession of democratic leaders, he speaks of Eucrates ὃς πρῶτος ἕξει τῆς πόλεως τὰ
πράγματα. τὰ πράγματα is used elsewhere of official power, and
it evidently imputes great influence to the προστάτης.

sibility, but his own theory of it is open to great
objection. From the fact that men of birth were
usually elected to the generalship, and from the
important part the demagogues took in criticizing
the administration, he developed the idea that the
προστάτης led the opposition to the government of
the rich oligarchs.

This theory is based in part on the false idea
that all opponents of the demagogues were of necessity oligarchs[1]. As a matter of fact the oligarchs
did not regularly take part in ordinary politics, and
men of known oligarchic sentiments even if elected
would have been rejected at the official examination (δοκιμασία); most of the generals even if not
keen democrats, were certainly not antidemocratic.
As I hope to show, the government, in the sense of
the chief executive magistracy, was the subject of
party contention and frequently changed hands. The
democrats proper (the war party) and the moderates
or middle party (usually inclining to peace) had a
fairly equal share of office. Hence it is obvious that
the leader of the demos was as often on the side of
the government as on that of the opposition, and
inasmuch as he could generally command the attention of the assembly, "leader of the house" would
be as fair a description of him as "leader of the
opposition."

The dema-　　Nor is it true that the demagogues were always

---

[1] Grote regards all men who do not act with the democrats as
oligarchs, even Nicias. See vol. vi. p. 65, "The principal person
of what may be called the oligarchical party." I have pointed
out in the last chapter that the middle party does not show any
trace of oligarchic leanings.

excluded from the generalship[1]. Pericles (who was *gogues and the generalship.* certainly προστάτης) held the generalship almost continuously. Of his successors[2], Eucrates was general for the year 432/1[3], at a time when he was doubtless a prominent member of his party, Lysicles in 428/7[4]. Cleon, apart from his extraordinary command in 425/4, was general in 424/3, and 422/1[5].

We do not know that Hyperbolus was ever elected to the generalship; his activity seems to have been employed in another sphere, but Alcibiades, who aspired to lead the demos, was eager for military command. Androcles, the demagogue, was probably general in 414/3[6]. Cleophon, who succeeded to him, is thought to have been general in 406/5, 405/4[7]. The lament of Eupolis for the good old days when generals came ἐκ τῶν μεγίστων οἰκιῶν[8] must refer to the admission of men of no birth to the generalship.

Naturally from their social position (which might

---

[1] This was also the view of Curtius, vol. iii. p. 88 (English Trans.), "Thus one of the most important changes that occurred at this time (after the death of Pericles) consisted in the separation of the office of general from that of popular leader."

[2] Ar. Eq. 128—38 gives Eucrates, Lysicles and Cleon as the three successors to Pericles.

[3] C. I. A. iv. 179. The general of that name, who is mentioned there, is probably identical with the demagogue.

[4] Thuc. iii. 19.

[5] For the first year, Ar. Nub. 581—94 is our authority; the inference is disputed, but see Beloch, Att. Pol. p. 305. For the second, Thuc. v. 1.

[6] So Beloch, Att. Pol. p. 63.

[7] For Cleophon, see Schol. to Ar. Ran. 679, Lys. 13. 12. The dates are uncertain; the evidence is discussed by Beloch, Rhein. Mus. xxxix. pp. 255—6.

[8] Frag. 117 (Kock).

have debarred men like Cleon and Cleophon from
continuous military training), as well as from the
time they spent in the assembly, the demagogues
were not so well qualified for active service as men
who made war their profession. They may have
usually stood for the generalship in order to gain a
share of the powers conferred by that office, but they
probably did not take the field so often as the military members of the board, and on this account we
do not find them mentioned so frequently in our
authorities.

*Combina-
tion of
military
power and
political
influence.*
We see then that the leading demagogue (who
was also the leading statesman of the democratic
party) often held military office; and this introduces
the consideration of a special position open to such
a man. When the office held was that of president
of the generals[1], and when it was continued for some
years, together with the favour and support of the
assembly, the holder was then not only "leader of
the house," but "first minister" (to apply modern
designations), and united in himself the chief civil
and military power, as well as the direction of state
policy.

This combination of official power and political
influence deserves especial consideration from the
possibilities it offered to ambitious men of practically
establishing a personal government. Democracies
and tyrannies have always been closely related, and
demagogues have frequently developed into tyrants[2].

[1] πρύτανις τῶν στρατηγῶν, see above p. 24.

[2] Aristot. Pol. 1305 a, 8 (ἐπὶ γὰρ τῶν ἀρχαίων, ὅτε γένοιτο ὁ
αὐτὸς δημαγωγὸς καὶ στρατηγός, εἰς τυραννίδα μετέβαλλον). Cf. Plato
Rep. viii. 565 D on the rise of the tyrant from the προστάτης.

From the unwieldy character of democracy, the *Democracy* difficulty of inducing a multitude to show energy in *and tyran-ny.* the pursuit of a consistent policy, and the possibilities of corruption and abuse, it often happens that the direction of state-affairs is entrusted to a dictator, who raises himself to power as the champion and deliverer of the sovereign people. Such a result may be achieved without revolution; a practical abrogation of the constitution under legal forms may take place by the conferment of almost autocratic power on a statesman; and at Athens we find such an informal tyranny established by more than one man.

To go into detail, the first essentials for this autocracy were the favour of the people and the command of the assembly, which were implied in the position of προστάτης τοῦ δήμου. The holder of this position acquired the requisite official power by becoming πρύτανις τῶν στρατηγῶν. To establish his authority firmly, nothing else was needed[1] but continuity, and this element was ensured by the habitual practice of reelecting the generals[2]. This combination of influence and power made the holder first and permanent minister of the state, as well as leading demagogue.

[1] The conferment of extraordinary powers on the general (στρατηγία αὐτοκράτωρ) was not necessary to this position, and was usually a temporary measure adopted for a particular expedition.

[2] Wilamowitz, Aus Kydathen, pp. 59 ff. says, " The possibility of a continuation of the generalship did away with the responsibility. For the reelected general, until the people reject him, there is no account to be rendered." He thinks there was only a nominal process of εὔθυναι before the θεσμοθέται. This is disputed, but in case of reelection it is probable that both εὔθυναι and δοκιμασία were little more than formal.

Pericles.   Such an autocracy was established by Pericles, during the period subsequent to the ostracism of Thucydides, son of Melesias. For he was general all this time[1], and in all probability president; he was also προστάτης, and had almost the sole direction of Athenian policy. We have good evidence that he possessed powers superior to those of ordinary magistrates[2], and Thucydides describes the constitution of the period as personal government under the forms of democracy[3].

Alcibiades.   The Athenians, in spite of their morbid fear of tyranny[4], were ready to submit to a legalized dictatorship, and the position won by Pericles was open to any man of sufficient ability and popularity. This possibility seems to offer a key to the career of Alcibiades, and to explain many actions of his, which otherwise seem hopelessly inconsistent. I believe that throughout his public life he was emulating Pericles, and that the position held by the latter formed his constant ideal. In two particulars he was immeasurably below Pericles as a statesman. Alcibiades was impatient of restraint and devoid of that moderation (σωφροσύνη)[5], which was so marked

    [1] Plut. Per. 16.
    [2] He is described in Thuc. twice as δέκατος αὐτὸς στρατηγός (see above, p. 22, n. 4). After his fall the people again (αὐτὸν) στρατηγὸν εἵλοντο καὶ πάντα τὰ πράγματα ἐπέτρεψαν (Thuc. ii. 65). Diod. xii. 42 describes Pericles as στρατηγὸς ὢν καὶ τὴν ὅλην ἡγεμονίαν ἔχων. The passage of Teleclides, quoted by Plut. Per. 16, probably refers to this position of his.
    [3] Thuc. ii. 65, ἐγίγνετο λόγῳ μὲν δημοκρατία, ἔργῳ δὲ ὑπὸ τοῦ πρώτου ἀνδρὸς ἀρχή.
    [4] Cf. the panic in 415, Thuc. vi. 53, 60.
    [5] See Vischer, Kleine Schriften, p. 106; Thuc. vi. 15 talks of his παρανομία.

a virtue in Pericles, while he substituted for the pure and highminded patriotism of the latter a selfish ambition for his personal advancement[1].

The democratic party could alone enable him to *His career.* reach the goal before him, and on this account he attached himself to it. Of his early life we know little, but we may conclude that, in spite of his temporary attempt to outbid Nicias for the Spartan προξενία[2], he began public life as a democrat[3]. His anti-Spartan policy was based on democratic traditions, and was urged in his own interests, as war would give him a chance of military distinction. He found himself thwarted by the influence of Nicias and by the even balance of parties in the state, and on this account he challenged ostracism. Fearing the result of this he combined with his chief political rival to get rid of Hyperbolus, who stood in his way as a competitor for the leadership of the demos.

For a time his influence was diminished, and to recover his former position he advocated the Sicilian expedition, which would, if carried to a successful issue, have assured him not only overwhelming popularity, but the military position and *prestige* necessary for his purpose. In fear of such an issue, the extreme democrats under Androcles, and the oligarchs under Thessalus, combined to overthrow him.

From 415 to 411 his plans were interrupted by his compulsory exile. After trying without success to establish his influence in Sparta and Persia by

[1] Plut. Alc. 2, τὸ φιλόνεικον καὶ τὸ φιλόπρωτον.

[2] Thuc. v. 43.

[3] The evidence is collected in Beloch, Att. Pol. p. 50. Cf. especially Thuc. vi. 89.

services rendered against Athens, he made his recall
the immediate object of his life. To secure this end
he was not scrupulous about the means employed,
and had no hesitation in working against the democracy. For his fall had been mainly due to the
democrats, and his return, while Androcles was chief
demagogue, was impossible. On these grounds he
initiated the oligarchic movement of 411, foreseeing
that his opportunity would come, as it did, in the
confusion caused by the revolution. He took this
step however from no love for the oligarchs, from
whom he broke as soon as possible, while they for
their part saw clearly enough that he was a man
" unfitted for oligarchy[1]."

Apparently the sincerity of his democratic professions was not doubted when he was recalled by
the army at Samos[2], and entrusted with supreme
power[3]. His advocacy of the rule of the 5000 was
entirely due to motives of expediency[4], as it started
a division in the ranks of the Four Hundred,
which was the cause of their overthrow; and the
restoration of full democracy in 410 was probably

[1] Thuc. viii. 63. Cf. also 68, and 70 (the oligarchs do not
recall the exiles because of Alcibiades).

[2] Thuc. viii. 81.

[3] Thuc. viii. 82, στρατηγὸν εἵλοντο...καὶ τὰ πράγματα πάντα
ἀνετίθεσαν. He had got the coveted position at Samos, and had
now only to have it confirmed at Athens.

[4] Thuc. viii. 86, ἀποκρινάμενος ὅτι...τοὺς μὲν πεντακισχιλίους
οὐ κωλύοι ἄρχειν. Some have thought on the strength of this passage that his ideal was a moderate democracy. This evidence in
itself is insufficient. Alcibiades found his chief support in the
fleet; and the fleet would have nothing to say to a limitation of
the franchise.

due to the fleet, in which Alcibiades' influence was paramount.

After this he proceeded cautiously ; he wished to strengthen his claim on Athens by military services, before taking advantage of his recall from banishment. When he did return, he came as the deliverer of Athens and the hope of the future, and at last it seemed as if the long desired reward was to be his. He had apparently been elected πρύτανις τῶν στρατηγῶν[1] before his return, he now had full powers conferred on him (ἀναρρηθεὶς ἁπάντων ἡγεμὼν αὐτοκράτωρ[2]). With some classes he enjoyed an unbounded popularity[3], and it only needed a continuance of popular favour and the successful conduct of the war on his part to give him a position in the state as strong as that of Pericles. But, before his power was firmly established, his enemies raised the charge that he was aiming at the tyranny, and this suspicion combined with his mismanagement of the war caused his final overthrow, and deprived Athens of the only man who of all her citizens might have effected her salvation.

I have summarized Alcibiades' career, because I *Aims of Alcibiades.* think the most satisfactory explanation of it is afforded by the supposition that he was striving to follow in Pericles' footsteps and establish a personal government on a constitutional basis.

It is usually assumed that his aim throughout life was to overthrow the democracy and establish

---

[1] See Beloch, Att. Pol. pp. 286—7, for a discussion of this.

[2] Xen. Hell. i. 4. 20, cf. Diod. xiii. 67, Plut. Alc. 33.

[3] Plut. Alc. 34 and 35.

himself as tyrant, that he was in the main equally
indifferent to oligarchy and democracy[1], while some
claim him as an adherent of the moderate democrats[2].
If the explanation I have suggested is right, the
object he pursued was perfectly legal and within the
constitution[3], and his consistency of purpose is evident through the apparent vacillation of his conduct.
He attached himself to democracy, not for its own
sake, but because his interests were bound up with
it, as the only form of government which could grant
his wishes; and for the democratic constitution and
party he worked, except for the interval of his banishment, throughout his life[4].

Lesser de-
magogues.   I have discussed the position of the leading demagogue, and the opportunity it offered him of at-

[1] As Phrynichus (Thuc. viii. 48) said. Thucydides endorses
the remark, and it may be true of Alcibiades' philosophic standpoint, but prudential motives attached him to democracy.

[2] Chiefly on the strength of Thuc. viii. 86, which I have discussed above, p. 58, n. 4.

[3] The suspicion was certainly entertained in 415 and 407 that
he was aiming at tyranny. (Thuc. vi. 15, Plut. Alc. 34—35.) The
very fact however that both in 415 when he might have appealed
to the army with a good hope of success, and in 407 when he had
so excellent an opportunity, he did not take the decisive step seems
to argue that he purposely avoided any illegal or revolutionary
method.

[4] This would explain the constant hatred of the oligarchs towards him, which is abundantly proved. On the other hand, the
other demagogues had no love for him. He was a man out of
sympathy with them, a rival claimant for the people's favour,
whose success would throw them completely into the shade. This
explains his conduct to Hyperbolus, the action of Androcles and
others. Thuc. ii. 65 refers to the rivalry of demagogues, in connection especially with the Sicilian expedition; vi. 15 he traces
his fall to the fear and envy of his greatness.

taining almost monarchic power; there were however many demagogues contented with a much
humbler position. These are usually cast into the
shade by the greater men, and so do not receive the
attention they deserve. Our authorities seldom
mention more than the leading demagogue; we cannot fill up the gaps, but we must not forget that
they only exist owing to the deficiency of our information, and were this complete we should see the
political stage crowded with figures.

The mention of a few names from Aristophanes
and other sources will give us some idea of these
lesser politicians. Pisander[1] (if he may be ranked
as a true democrat) is the constant object of Aristophanes' abuse. Hyperbolus[2] appears in Aristophanes
long before the historians mention him. We hear
of Theorus, Aeschines and Phanus[3] as three com-
panions of Cleon, who were probably humble politicians, of Thudippus who proposed the raising of
the tribute[4], of Demostratus who took a prominent
part in advocating the Sicilian expedition[5]. From
Andocides we hear of Demophantus proposing a
democratic oath, probably on the restoration of full
democracy in 410[6]; from Lysias of Cleisthenes,
Epigenes, Demophanes as active democrats in 410[7],
and from Xenophon of Archedemus, Timocrates

[1] Babyl. fr. 81 (Kock), Pax 395, Lys. 490.
[2] Ach. 846, Eq. 1303, Nub. 623.
[3] Ar. Vesp. 1220, cf. Ach. 134, Eq. 1256.
[4] C. I. A. i. 37.
[5] Ar. Lys. 391.
[6] Andoc. 1. 96.
[7] Lys. 25. 25.

and Callixenus as prosecutors of the generals in 406[1].

This list, incomplete as it is, will suffice to show at once how many active politicians there must have been, and how little we know of them.

Sphere of the demagogues. Demagogy was a profession, with a method and sphere of its own. The object of it was to protect the interests and to gain the favour of the people by zealous devotion to their service. There were three places in which the demagogue could do this, the public assembly, the council, and the law courts. Of these the assembly was the most important. All business of state was under its control, by it the policy of the commonwealth was decided, the administration was carried on and the magistrates were criticized and directed. In proportion to the importance of the assembly the power of the orator rose, and oratory was an essential part of the demagogic art[2]. The business side of the demagogue's duty in the assembly was to propose and support the decrees, in which all state business was embodied, and hence the ψήφισμα was regarded as his special weapon[3].

Any business introduced in the assembly required

---

[1] Xen. Hell. i. 7. For Archedemus cf. also Ar. Ran. 420.

[2] The importance of oratory appears in the prominence given by Thucydides to the speeches of public men, and in the complaints of Pericles and Cleon that the people allow themselves to be carried away by oratory. Cf. Thuc. ii. 43, iii. 38. In Ar. Eq. 860 Cleon says to Demos μὴ τοῦ λέγοντος ἴσθι. Possibly this was a constant reproach of Cleon's, but it may be a reminiscence of the actual speech reported by Thucydides l. c.

[3] Cf. Ar. Eq. 1383, Nub. 1428, Aves, 1035, and see Gilbert, Beiträge, p. 79.

the previous sanction of the council, and on this account it was necessary for the democrats to be well represented there. The lesser men of the party and the rising demagogues tried to get a place on it. Possibly the competition for a seat there was not very keen, and in spite of the uncertainty of the lot many of the demagogues, including Cleon[1], Hyperbolus[2] and Androcles[3], were members of the council at some period of their career.

Coming to the actual part taken by the dema- *Finance.* gogues in political affairs, there are some subjects in which they took a special interest and displayed particular activity. These were the administration of finance, the criticism and prosecution of magistrates, and the prosecution of suspected oligarchs. Legislation on financial matters belonged to the assembly, administration to the council[4], while we have seen that the generals, also, had some financial duties. Failing a post on the board of generals or on the council, the demagogues' influence must have been unofficial; but in some way nearly all demagogues concerned themselves with finance. As Böckh[5] say:—"Some statesmen occupied themselves with it exclusively; and all the great demagogues endeavoured to obtain either direct or indirect influence over it." Pericles is known to have con-

---

[1] Ar. Eq. 774 (Cleon says ἦνίκ' ἐβούλευον) refers probably to a fact. Cf. Gilbert, Beiträge, p. 82, Beloch, Att. Pol. p. 335.

[2] According to Gilbert, Beiträge, p. 81.

[3] Andoc. 1. 27 (Androcles appears as acting on behalf of the βουλή).

[4] Böckh, i. 183.

[5] ib.

trolled the financial as well as the general policy of
Athens. Cleon[1] followed his example. Cleophon,
who in many ways was Cleon's political heir, devoted
his attention to finance, and for years took a leading
part in financial administration, apparently with great
success[2].

Criticism and prose-cution of magis-trates. The demagogue also undertook the censure and
if necessary the prosecution of inefficient or corrupt
magistrates. The assembly must have been the frequent scene of complaints against official mismanagement, and here Cleon criticized Nicias' conduct in the
command at Pylos[3]. The demagogues did not always
confine themselves to criticism, and the prosecution
of generals was constant.

The idea that power involved responsibility was

---

[1] Ar. Eq. 774 (on the βουλή). Gilbert, Beiträge, pp. 133—42,
thinks Ach. 5 refers to an endeavour of Cleon's to reduce the κατά-
στασις of the knights. For his financial policy see below, pp. 70
and 73. He is credited with the raising of the tribute and of the
dicast's fee.

[2] Lys. 19. 48, πολλὰ ἔτη διεχείρισε τὰ τῆς πόλεως, ib. 21. 3.
The first passage seems to refer so explicitly to a definite office,
that Beloch (Rhein. Mus. xxxix. pp. 249—259) has argued that
Cleophon must have been president of the board of πορισταί
(which we know to have existed in this period), and that this
office was instituted in 413 to control the whole financial administration. This is perhaps supported by Thuc. viii. 1, τῶν τε κατὰ
τὴν πόλιν τι ἐς εὐτέλειαν σωφρονίσαι, which might be taken as a
vague description of this reform. Such an indirect allusion would
be quite characteristic of Thucydides, as he does not mention the
appointment of the πρόβουλοι directly, but refers to ἀρχή τις
πρεσβυτέρων ἀνδρῶν. Against the theory Ar. Lys. 421 may perhaps be urged, where the πρόβουλος speaks of himself as having
the duties which this theory assigns to the πορισταί.

[3] Thuc. iv. 27, 28. Cf. Ar. Eq. 288 (διαβαλῶ σ' ἐὰν στρατηγῇς),
and 355, 358, which evidently refer to this.

accepted and carried out with the utmost completeness in Athens. If a magistrate accepted the trust he did so with the knowledge that his failure if in any degree culpable would be visited with severe punishment ; as a matter of fact failure in any case was too often followed by prosecution[1].

Hence there is an almost continuous series of prosecutions directed against generals, nearly all of which may be traced to the action of the democrats. Pericles, Phormio, Paches, Eurymedon, Pythodorus, Sophocles, Thucydides, Eucles, Phrynichus and Scironides, and the conquerors of Arginusae all suffered condemnation. Demosthenes, Nicias and Alcibiades preferred to escape popular resentment by absenting themselves from Athens. Laches alone serves to prove that an Athenian law court could acquit an unsuccessful general[2].

The demagogue also employed his talents in bringing to trial those who were suspected of oligarchic designs and conspiracy against the constitution. The Athenians lived in constant fear of such plots, and probably had good reason for their suspicions, as the oligarchs were thoroughly disloyal to the constitution. We can infer from Aristophanes[3]

Prosecution of suspected oligarchs.

---

[1] Magistrates were frequently prosecuted on standing their εὔθυναι (cf. Ar. Eq. 259, 825), but it is disputed whether generals had to submit to any real account. See above, p. 55, n. 2.

[2] This is not the place to discuss how far the condemnations were justified. In cases where we have reliable information, as in that of Thucydides, we see that there was strong evidence against the generals. In spite of the risk of condemnation the office of general was eagerly sought after.

[3] Cf. Equites 235, 257, 278, 452, 475 ; Vesp. 344, 488. In the last passage Bdelycleon says,

W. 5

the frequency with which such charges were bandied about, and the history of events after the mutilation of the Hermae and the revolution of 411 shows how eagerly the demagogues undertook the exposure of conspiracies and the prosecution of treason.

This prosecution was not confined to citizens. Suspected allies were summoned to Athens and put on trial for similar charges of treason[1]. As I have argued above, in most cases where the allies were prosecuted in Athens, the prosecutions were for political offences, and the discontent of the oligarchs, attested by every revolt from the confederation, shows that there was just ground for the charges.

The prosecution of magistrates and of suspected oligarchs was properly a political duty undertaken by the demagogues. Some of them paid especial attention to the law courts, and probably many of the younger democrats won their spurs in this way[2] This will account for the frequency of the charges of συκοφαντία[3] brought against the demagogues. The

ὡς ἅπανθ' ὑμῖν τυραννίς ἐστι καὶ ξυνωμόται
ἤν τε μεῖζον ἤν τ' ἔλαττον πρᾶγμα τις κατηγορῇ.

Cf. also Plato Rep. viii. 565 B (from the frequency of charges of oligarchic conspiracy, men are forced against their will into being oligarchs).

[1] Cf. Resp. Ath. passim, discussed above, p. 29 n. 2, Ar. Pax 640. The passages in Aristophanes in which the demagogues are represented as having power over the allies probably refer to this. Eq. 170, Pax 642, &c.

[2] Cf. Ar. Ach. 680 (young orators prosecute old men). The law courts were Hyperbolus' special sphere of action, Ach. 846.

[3] This word implies a professional prosecutor who hopes to gain honour and reward by threatened prosecution, or at least to be bought off by his threatened victim.

accusation must have had a substantial basis in fact,
and there were probably many utterly unscrupulous
characters who used such methods of intimidation;
but without definite evidence it is impossible to say
how far the leading demagogues were guilty[1].

Having considered the composition of the democratic party and the character of the leaders under
whom it was organized, we have still to consider the
chief points in its policy. It is usually assumed
that politics and politicians changed for the worse
after Pericles. There was cause enough for degeneracy in the plague, perpetual war and financial
difficulty, but it is possible to exaggerate the actual
effects. Curtius[2] gives a picture which is too highly
coloured. "The age was degenerate....A discontented and turbulent mob was formed in Athens,
craving for excitement, idle and overbusy, babbling
and curious. A new demagogy sprang into ex-

Supposed degeneracy of the democracy.

---

[1] The Athenian law courts from their organization laboured
under the disadvantage of being open to political appeals, and it
would be possible to represent every prosecution for political
offences as a malicious attack on opponents. Müller-Strübing,
Aristophanes, p. 355, thinks that every attempt to constrain the
magistrates to observe the laws was described as συκοφαντία, and
that the action of the demagogues in this respect was innocent and
praiseworthy. We do not know that συκοφαντία was limited to one
party. The oligarchs may have endeavoured to use it against their
opponents. Lys. 12. 4 calls the Thirty πονηροὶ καὶ συκοφάνται, and
the ξυνωμοσίαι ἐπὶ δίκαις may not have been entirely defensive. On
the other hand the Athenian courts were at this date apparently
singularly free from corruption. So also in all probability were
the orators. No definite evidence can be brought against them,
and we have positive testimony in the case of Cleophon of his
innocence, Lys. 19. 48.

[2] Vol. iii. pp. 81—3 (English Trans.).

5—2

istence. Pericles' successors were the people's servants and flatterers."

There is in the above description this amount of truth that there was no one like Pericles to succeed him. The talents which Pericles possessed were not found united in any other man. As a consequence political life was not kept at the high level at which it had been before; and men of less refinement took the lead[1], partly no doubt because the development of democracy had opened up a career to all and extended political education, partly because there were no great statesmen in the ranks of birth and wealth. But though this imported a certain amount of coarseness and passion into political life, we must be careful to distinguish between the character of the politicians and their aims. While we may admit a change in the method pursued, there was, except in one particular, no great change of policy.

Objects of the democrats. The democrats throughout the war always kept two great objects in view, to defend the democracy and to maintain the empire. This purpose is referred to by the author of the work on " the Athenian Constitution," when he says that, " the demos do not wish to live as subjects in a well ordered city but to be free and rule[2];" and the watchwords of democracy and empire appear no less prominently in the funeral oration of Pericles[3]. To the maintenance of the democracy and the alliance, as I have argued above, the continuance of the war was regarded as indis-

[1] Cf. Ar. Eq. 191 (an implied comparison between Pericles and Cleon).

[2] i. 8.

[3] Thuc. ii. 36 and 37.

pensable. We thus arrive at three principles of democratic policy which were inseparably connected. The democrats were determined to defend the democracy, to maintain the alliance, and on this account to prosecute the war with all possible vigour to a decisive end. These principles Cleon and his successors held in common with Pericles, and it was only in the application of them that they neglected his advice.

The objects of the democrats fall naturally into the two divisions of home and foreign policy. On the first head little need be said. It is a statement which requires no proof, that the democrats were attached to the democracy, and the history of the period shows how ready they were to defend it against every attack. There was only one interval during which the constitution was modified and the change was abnormal and temporary. The reforms of 413 were the inevitable result of a reaction against extreme democracy, which was regarded as responsible for the Sicilian disaster. The reforms then introduced prepared the way for the revolution of 411. This was only effected in the absence of a large number of the citizens keenly attached to the democracy, and by a system of terrorism and assassination which stifled all opposition. The oligarchy of the Four Hundred was an unnatural product, and was soon superseded by a mixed constitution, which only served as an intermediate step to the restoration of full democracy.[1]

Defence of the democracy.

---

[1] There is no direct testimony for this restoration, except perhaps the psephism of Demophantus. The point, though long

The di-cast's fee.

There is one point in particular in which we can trace the consistent effort of the democrats to defend the constitution in all its principles. It is in the resolve to maintain the system of paid jury courts. The jury fee was in itself neither a heavy charge on the revenue[1], nor sufficient to compete with the remuneration of ordinary labour. It was a partial compensation to the dicast for his sacrifice of time. As such it was absolutely necessary to the system of large jury courts, which were regarded as an essential part of the democratic constitution. Without some compensation it would have been impossible to induce a sufficient number of citizens to undertake judicial duties. The abuse lavished on this fee was doubtless meant for the institution which required it, and it is obvious that without it the system of popular jurisdiction must have broken down.

About 425 this fee was raised from two to three obols, and the increase, which in all probability was proposed by Cleon[2], was occasioned by the general rise of prices consequent on the war[3]. In 411 all

disputed, has been established in detail by Vischer, Kleine Schriften, pp. 205—38, and is scarcely any longer a matter of doubt.

[1] At its highest when the fee was three obols (425—411) it was not more than 150 talents. This amount is derived from Ar. Vesp. 660, which Fränkel regards as absurdly exaggerated (see above, p. 44, n. 1). Beloch (Rhein. Mus. xxxix. p. 244) thinks the total amount required for the three obol fee was about 100 talents, of which about a third came from the court fees, while from 410 onwards, after the revolt of the allies, for a two obol fee scarcely more than 33 talents were required.

[2] This appears from Ar. Eq. 255.

[3] Müller-Strübing, Aristophanes, pp. 149—157. It was rendered possible by the increase of the φόρος, which took place about the same time. See below, p. 72.

state payments were abolished by the oligarchs, and the powers of the jury courts passed to the council. We do not know what arrangements were made for the next year or two[1]; but after the overthrow of oligarchy, perhaps simultaneously with the return to full democracy, as soon as the measure was financially possible, the pay was restored; apparently at the lower fee of two obols[2]. This is sufficient to show the importance attached by the democrats to popular jury courts and to the system of pay which alone rendered them possible.

The foreign policy of the democrats includes two *Foreign* subjects, closely connected with one another, the *policy* alliance and the war[3]. With reference to these *of the democrats.* Pericles had carefully marked out the policy he considered essential to success in three principles[4]. The first was to make no concession to Sparta, to conclude no peace that did not leave Athens mistress of the situation[5]. The second was to keep a strict hand over the allies, for herein was the source of Athenian power (and, as a corollary to this, to pay attention to the fleet and avoid land engagements)[6]. The third was to attempt no fresh conquests[7]. It was in the last

[1] During the moderate democracy of 411—10 powers of government including probably judicial administration were entrusted to men of hoplite census, who of course did not need the dicast's fee.

[2] Ar. Ran. 1466, quoted by Beloch, ib. p. 239, and discussed by him.

[3] The relation of the democrats (and the other political parties) to the war is discussed at length in the next chapter.

[4] See Oncken, Athen und Hellas, i. pp. 302—7.

[5] μὴ εἴκειν Πελοποννησίοις, Thuc. i. 140—141.

[6] τὰ τῶν ξυμμάχων διὰ χειρὸς ἔχειν, Thuc. ii. 13; cf. i. 143.

[7] ἀρχὴν μὴ ἐπικτᾶσθαι. Thuc. i. 144; cf. Plut. Per. 20.

point only that his advice was disregarded; the other two principles were upheld without compromise by Cleon and his successors against Nicias and his party.

Treatment of the allies. In their conduct to the allies the democrats were certainly following the rules laid down by Pericles; but they carried out those rules with unnecessary harshness and brutality. This appears in their proposed treatment of Mytilene, their actual treatment of Chios and Scione, as well as in their action towards Thera and Melos.

The general attitude of the democrats to the allies has been already discussed[1]; they maintained that the relation was one of tyrant and subject, and to a certain extent they realized their theory. For the present, however, there is one important measure, affecting the allies, which requires attention.

Raising of the tribute. The tribute of the allies, which at the beginning of the period did not exceed 600 talents[2], was at some later period doubled. For this fact there has always been satisfactory authority[3], but the date

---

[1] See above, chapter I. p. 26.

[2] Thuc. ii. 13. Diod. xii. 40 (from another source) and [Andoc.] 4. 11 give the tribute as 460 talents at this time. Inscriptions support them, and Beloch (Rhein. Mus. xxxix. pp. 35 ff.) thinks that Diodorus is right, and that, while he gives the φόρος only, Thucydides is reckoning the total receipts from the allies, including indirect taxation and the toll from the Bosporus.

[3] Andoc. 3. 9, Aesch. F. L. 337, both say that more than 1200 talents came in yearly during the peace of Nicias. Plut. Arist. 24 wrongly says that the tribute was *gradually* raised to 1300 talents by the demagogues. Cf. also Ar. Vesp. 655 ff., where the total revenue of Athens is put at 2000 talents, pointing to a large increase. Grote, v. p. 269, n. 2, argued that these passages were

was not known until the examination of inscriptions proved conclusively that it took place in the year 425[1].

The many passages in the Equites[2], in which Aristophanes dwells on the oppression of the allies, point to some such measure, and evidently bring it into connection with Cleon and his party. The actual proposer, Thudippus, is an unknown man and can only have acted as the agent of the democrats; one statement[3], in itself of very doubtful authority, makes Alcibiades the moving spirit; but though he doubtless supported the proposal, and may have been on the commission of assessment, it is probable that he did not take a leading part. Cleon was fresh from his triumph at Pylus, and was then at the height of his power. There can scarcely be a doubt that he was responsible for it[4].

Whatever view we may take of the justice of this step, it was absolutely necessary. The expenses of *The increase a necessity.* war[5], which may usually be regarded as extraordinary, had become permanent; the reserves had been exhausted, and Athens had herself to submit to a property tax (εἰσφορά). In addition to this it had been determined to take the offensive against Sparta, and it may have seemed that the need for the increase would be only temporary.

---

not sufficient to outweigh the silence of Thucydides; but their substantial accuracy is established by Köhler's investigations.

[1] Köhler, Abhand. der Akad. Berl., 1869, pp. 142—53.
[2] 313, 802, 1034; cf. Vesp. 671.
[3] [Andoc.] 4. 11.
[4] Köhler, ib. p. 151.
[5] See below (chap. IV.) on the financial history of the war.

The amount not excessive.   The amount in itself does not seem excessive. If Athens alone raised a tax of 200 talents, a sum of 1100 or 1200 talents was not out of proportion for the whole of the allies. If we may assume that the allies felt the confederation to be for their interest, it was just that they should make pecuniary sacrifices in return for the active service undertaken by Athens.

It is also possible that the increase did not involve any violation of the original terms of the alliance arranged by Aristides. We know that the league was gradually extended, that the number of members in the alliance in 476 was far smaller than it was after the Persians had been driven from the Aegean, and that many states which originally supplied ships subsequently contributed money[1]. Moreover we have the explicit testimony of Thucydides[2] that the original contribution amounted to 460 talents.

To produce this amount the states then in the alliance must have paid at a higher rate, than they did later; and as time went on and fresh states joined the confederation, we find that the total

---

[1] The original extent of the league is a matter in dispute. Kirchhoff (Hermes, xi. pp. 1 ff.) argues that the league owed its great extension to the battle of Eurymedon. In this he is followed by Fränkel (n. 626 to Böckh). Beloch (Rhein. Mus. xliii. pp. 104 ff.) attacks this theory, but it cannot be disputed that the league gained many new members in the fifth century.

[2] i. 96. Kirchhoff (ib. p. 30) regards this amount as impossible. In this opinion he is followed by many historians (Busolt, Griech. Gesch. ii. p. 352, Gilbert, Handbuch, i. p. 396). Kirchhoff's explanation of the passage in Thucydides is not satisfactory, nor is it safe to regard it as an interpolation, as Diod. xi. 47, Plut. Arist. 24, and Nep. Arist. 3 are in agreement with Thucydides.

revenue was not increased, and individual contributions were lowered[1]. Thus the tribute of those
states which had contributed from the first must
in time have been considerably reduced, and the
increase of 425 may only have restored the average
rate of the original assessment[2].

It is hard to apportion fairly the burden of taxation between different classes or different parts of an
empire; it is probable that, considering the military
exertions of Athens, she had more to bear than the
allies, and did not get a fair return for the sacrifices
she made[3].

In their war policy the democrats were at one *War*
with Pericles in insisting on an active prosecution of *policy*
of the
the war and refusing all concession to Sparta. They *democrats.*
regarded the feud as irreconcileable, and hence when
Athens was in a position to impose terms they would
only have such as would place Sparta at a permanent
disadvantage[4], and when the course of the war was

[1] Fränkel, n. 629. The quota lists show that the rate of tribute
was lowered in 450 and 446.

[2] I have omitted to consider the change in the method of
levying the tribute, effected by the introduction of the εἰκοστή in
413. We know neither the motives for nor the effects of this
change, and have not much ground for regarding it as a part of the
democratic policy.

[3] Cf. Wilamowitz, Aus Kydathen, pp. 27, 28. "The value
of money was overestimated (i.e. in allowing the allies to purchase
immunity from service). Athenians of means contributed at a
higher rate than the allies, and the charge that Athens exacted
more than she needed is untrue." Cf. Plut. Per. 12 (Pericles
argued that the Athenians owed nothing to the allies, whom they
protected from Persia without calling upon them for service).

[4] They were not content to return to the *status quo;* Athens
was to be in a position of definite superiority to Sparta. Hence

unfavourable to Athens they would consent to no peace which involved the slightest diminution of Athenian power.

But in their desire to crush Sparta, they neglected Pericles' advice as to the plan of war to be followed; they carried the war into the enemy's camp by vigorous land campaigns, and endeavoured by alliance and by distant conquest to strengthen themselves against the foe.

Plan of war.

In the first place they were not satisfied with the purely defensive system of Pericles. They would not wait for Sparta to be weary of war, they wanted to inflict injury on her and reduce her to submission. Hence they effected the blockade of the Peloponnesus, and attempted the investment of Boeotia, which ended so disastrously at Delium.

Alliance with Argos.

From the same motive they sought alliance with the enemies of Sparta, in order to strengthen themselves against her. Argos had been Sparta's great rival in the Peloponnesus; she had formerly been allied with Athens against Sparta, and was the most powerful democracy in Greece next to Athens. There was therefore every motive for an alliance between these two powers. The truce between Argos and Sparta prevented any immediate action; but in all probability Athens anticipated its expiry, and the democrats made overtures to Argos[1]. These over-

---

after Pylos πλείονος, μειζόνων ὠρέγοντο (Thuc. iv. 21, 41). The terms Cleon demanded in 425 would have made Athens as a land power almost a match for Sparta.

[1] Ar. Eq. 464—5, speaking of Cleon, οὔκουν μ' ἐν Ἀργείοις ἃ πράττει λανθάνει | πρόφασιν μὲν Ἀργείους ἡμῖν ποιεῖ κ.τ.λ. This probably had some foundation in fact; see Gilbert, Beiträge,

tures were not however carried to any conclusion, and the accession of the peace party to power in 421 and the alliance with Sparta defeated this project. As soon as Athens and Sparta began to draw apart, Alcibiades pressed on the alliance with Argos, and from that time (with the interval of the oligarchic revolution at Argos) Athens found in her a true ally.

The desire of the Athenians for the extension of the empire, connected with their wish to strengthen themselves against Sparta, led not only to the attacks on Thera and Melos, but to the fatal Sicilian expedition. This project, which arose from the arrogant assumption that Athens, as mistress of the sea, should include within her dominion all islands inhabited by Greeks, had been mooted in the time of Pericles[1]. Athens had real interests in Sicily[2], to protect which she sent forces thither as early as 427, and her interference had been constant down to the year 424. The expedition of 415 was the resumption of a previous plan on a larger scale, and owing to the fact that Athens was not actually engaged in war[3] elsewhere its prospects seemed favourable. The proposal was probably due to the ambition of Alcibiades; but when once started, it met with enthusi-

The Sicilian expedition.

188—90. The approaching expiry of the truce was a great motive with Sparta for the conclusion of the war.

[1] Plut. Per. 20.

[2] If the Ionians succumbed to the Dorians, the latter might send aid to Sparta (as they did after 413), Thuc. iii. 86. Cf. ii. 7. It is important to remember that commercial interests were involved in the expedition. Many merchants sailed with it in the hopes of making a profit (Thuc. vi. 31), and the conquest of Sicily would have caused a vast extension of Athenian trade.

[3] Except in Thrace.

astic support. The only opposition, which must have been of a very half-hearted character, came from Nicias and his following; and though all sections of the population were eager for it, the democratic party must bear the responsibility.

The conquest of Sicily was no impossible feat. The failure of the attempt was due to incompetence and mismanagement on the Athenian side, combined with the greatest skill and courage on the part of their opponents[1]. But admitting that the prospect was good, the expedition was a great blunder from the democratic stand-point. The struggle with Sparta had not been fought out, a renewal of the contest was inevitable, and Athens was doing what she could to hasten it.

Had her force not been wasted in Sicily she would have been a match for Sparta when the struggle was renewed. But for this misguided piece of aggression, the democratic policy was as sane as it was consistent. Their constant effort was to maintain the constitution and the alliance, and on this account to offer an uncompromising resistance to Sparta, whose hostility threatened both.

---

[1] Thuc. ii. 65 says the Sicilian expedition was not an error of judgment, but failed because those at home did not, owing to political dissensions, take proper measures to support it. It is hard to see to what he refers, as the Athenians sent overwhelming forces to Sicily. The loss of Alcibiades, and the action he took in obtaining help for Syracuse, were of great effect, but Nicias was really to blame. Thucydides' narrative makes it painfully evident that he missed every possible occasion, that Syracuse (and with it Sicily) might have been speedily reduced, and that his early mistakes might have been repaired by a slight display of energy.

§ 2.   The Oligarchical Party.

In the general obscurity and uncertainty of the
political history of Athens the democratic party and
its policy appear to us in comparative distinctness
owing to the prominence given to them by the contemporary authorities. Of the other political sections
we have not such definite information, and we are
therefore reduced to inference and conjecture, so
that our knowledge is both less complete and less
reliable.

A feeling of opposition to an extreme democracy *Opposition*
must have been excited in the minds of many Athe- *to democ-*
racy en-
nians, and to this feeling the education of the day *couraged*
by the
contributed not a little. Aristotle insists on the *philosophy*
importance of the adaptation of general education *of the day.*
to the constitution[1]; but at Athens the teaching of
the philosophers was directly antagonistic to the existing government.

The Athenian constitution depended on the sovereignty of law[2], and there was a tendency to overestimate the value of institutions, which were regarded
as sacred and almost perfect: the philosophy of the
period, on the contrary, was sceptical, took nothing
for granted, and put every institution on its trial.

The caricature of Aristophanes[3] is equally appli-
cable to the Sophists or to Socrates:

---

[1] Αr. Pol. 1310 a, 12 μέγιστον δὲ πάντων πρὸς τὸ διαμένειν τὰς
πολιτείας...τὸ παιδεύεσθαι πρὸς τὰς πολιτείας.

[2] Wilamowitz, Aus Kydathen, pp. 47 ff.

[3] Nub. 1399—1400.

ὡς ἡδὺ καινοῖς πράγμασιν καὶ δεξιοῖς ὁμιλεῖν, καὶ τῶν καθεστώτων νόμων ὑπερφρονεῖν δύνασθαι.

While Socrates[1] contrasted the existing constitution with the ideal state of his philosophy, and found it wanting, the Sophists[2], so far as we can attribute to them any unity of thought, decried the acceptance of anything on tradition and exalted the individual above the state.

Both brought the blemishes of the constitution into prominence without proposing any positive or practical reform. The consequence was that while many regarded the constitution with critical eyes, but were content to put up with it, others found in this teaching a justification of their own feelings against the democracy, and made it their one political object to attack or undermine it. From this class came most of the oligarchic leaders.

The oligarchs a disloyal faction.

The oligarchs as a whole were a disloyal faction[3],

[1] Cf. Vischer, Kleine Schriften, i. p. 102. "Socrates' influence was not of a nature to form practical statesmen. His just discontent with the existing democracy, and his method of criticizing everything, had the effect of teaching his pupils the defects of the state and making them estimate it lightly, without positive results. No good Athenian statesman of importance came from his acquaintance, but many a mischievous one." See also Hertzberg, Alkibiades, pp. 33—36, and Grote, viii. p. 198, on Plato.

[2] Cf. Vischer, ib. p. 155. "The principle that the individual exists only in the state is reversed, the state is now the tool to give power and weight to the individual will." Cf. Müller-Strübing, Aristophanes, p. 244. This exaltation of the individual was the result of the general philosophic movement of which the Sophists were the representatives.

[3] They come under Bolingbroke's definition, "National interests would be sometimes sacrificed and always made subordinate

for neither their methods nor their objects entitle them to be regarded as a party. They not only rejected the obligation to obey the laws, but they were traitors to their country, for they intrigued with the national enemy against it; their ends were always selfish and treasonable, and were pursued by means of conspiracy and terrorism.

They formed, as their name[1] implies, a small minority of the state, and were for the most part men of wealth[2], or political adventurers who saw possibilities of their own advancement in the chance of revolution. In particular many of the young aristocrats[3], who looked with contempt on the rule of the lower classes, and were anxious to overthrow it, joined their ranks.

The motives which put the rich men in opposition to the constitution are obvious. Political struggles in most states are between the privileged few and the excluded many, who suffer from

Natural discontent of the rich.

---

to personal interests; and that, I think, is the true characteristic of faction."

[1] ὀλίγοι, the most general title.

[2] For the natural opposition of the rich to the democracy and its policy, which I have discussed above, there is direct evidence. Thuc. viii. 47, 48 (the trierarchs and rich men wish to get power into their own hands); ib. 63 (they resolve to go on with the revolution ὡς οὐκέτι ἄλλοις ἢ σφίσιν αὐτοῖς ταλαιπωροῦντας); ib. 65 (the exclusion of the poorer classes from power was their great object). Cf. Xen. Hell. ii. 4, 40 (Thrasybulus addresses the supporters of the Thirty, ὑμεῖς δὲ πλουσιώτεροι πάντων ὄντες πολλὰ καὶ αἰσχρὰ ἕνεκα κερδέων πεποιήκατε). These passages suffice to prove the connection between the richer classes and the oligarchs.

[3] The Knights were regarded as champions of anti-democratic feeling. Cf. Ar. Equites. They supported the Four Hundred (Thuc. viii. 92), and the Thirty (Xen. Hell. iii. 1, 4, Lys. 16).

the oppression of the government, or wish to reform
it in the direction of equality. Athens had, however,
passed out of this stage, and the political conflict
was reactionary, the rich striving to regain the
powers they had lost and to protect themselves from
the oppression of the ruling poor.

At one time the rich alone had been qualified for
high office, and had controlled the government in
their own interests; they had then been ready to
make sacrifices in order to enjoy these privileges,
and to contribute to the revenue in proportion to
their wealth. Now, while their burdens had increased, their privileges had vanished. They had
seen the basis of government gradually widened, and
at every step had vainly attempted by any means to
prevent the change.

They felt a natural resentment against a constitution, under which they not only had to support the
burdens of the state, the property-tax, the trierarchy
and other liturgies, but had the additional grievance[1]
that for all their sacrifices they got no return, and
had not a whit more power than the meanest citizen.

History of the oligarchical party. Hence they had always been at war with the
democracy which had brought this to pass, and the
motives under which they acted in 411, were the
same as their motives in 479, when, as Plutarch[2]

---

[1] Cf. Ar. Pol. 1295 b, 13, οἱ μὲν ἐν ὑπεροχαῖς εὐτυχημάτων ὄντες,
ἰσχύος καὶ πλούτου καὶ φίλων καὶ τῶν ἄλλων τῶν τοιούτων, ἄρχεσθαι
οὔτε βούλονται οὔτε ἐπίστανται. Cf. with this Thuc. iii. 45, ἡ δ'
ἐξουσία ὕβρει τὴν πλεονεξίαν (παρέχουσα) καὶ φρονήματι. Ar. Pol.
1303 b, 6 is still more appropriate, ἐν δὲ ταῖς δημοκρατίαις (στασιά-
ζουσιν) οἱ γνώριμοι ὅτι μετέχουσι τῶν ἴσων οὐκ ἴσοι ὄντες.

[2] Plut. Arist. 13; cf. Müller-Strübing, Aristophanes, pp. 244 ff.

tells us, men of noble families and great property, becoming impoverished by the war, and seeing their political power and reputation in the state vanishing, while others got the honours and controlled the government, conspired against the democracy.

This attitude they maintained throughout the fifth century, opposing the progress of democracy both by legitimate methods and by conspiracy; but after the ostracism of Thucydides open opposition was abandoned for intrigue[1]. Henceforth their objects were treasonable, and this circumstance shaped both their action and their organization.

They could not openly advocate their proposals, *Organiza-* but had either to withdraw altogether from political *tion of this* life, as many of them did, or dissemble their convic- *party.* tions[2], and under the guise of democrats work against democracy. For the same reason their political associations were in the first place secret, and in the second place separate, for combination would have brought suspicion on them.

For this purpose they combined in political clubs *Oligarchic* called ἑταιρεῖαι[3]. Politicians of all parties seem *Clubs.* to have adopted organizations of this nature to strengthen their position, but they were especially favoured by the oligarchs. Their original purpose seems to have been mainly defensive: the men who

---

[1] See above, p. 37.

[2] Beloch, Att. Pol. p. 13.

[3] For these see Vischer, Kleine Schriften, i. pp. 153—204, who collects all the available information on this subject, and endeavours to trace their influence on history. See also Scheibe, Die oligarchische Umwälzung, p. 5. They are called ξυνωμοσίαι in Thuc. viii. 54.

gathered this band of helpers round them used their
assistance in law-suits and elections[1]; and as oligarchs
were especially liable to prosecution, and as they
needed close organization to compensate for their
deficiency of numbers, these clubs came to be regarded
in time as oligarchic institutions, although they were
not confined to one party[2]. Of their constitution we
know little: they were naturally secret[3]; many of
the clubs were centred round a single individual[4], to
whose interests they were devoted; and though
usually independent of each other[5], they might be
united, whenever there seemed a good opportunity
of taking steps to carry their wishes into effect.
Thus the oligarchic clubs, if not essentially treasonable, were adapted to treasonable ends[6].

Con-
nection of
these

It is probable that these associations were kept

[1] Thuc. l. c. ξυνωμοσίαι ἐπὶ δίκαις καὶ ἀρχαῖς.   Cf. Plato Theaet.
173 D, ἑταιρεῖαι ἐπ᾽ ἀρχάs.

[2] Thus Pericles, Nicias and Alcibiades each had his hetaery,
see Vischer, ib. pp. 163, 169, 174.

[3] Plato Rep. ii. 365 D, ἐπὶ γὰρ τὸ λανθάνειν ξυνωμοσίας τε καὶ
ἑταιρείας ξυνάξομεν.

[4] Thus we hear of the hetaeries of Phaeax, Euphiletus, Alcibiades, &c.

[5] Thuc. viii. 54 (Pisander induced the clubs to combine ὅπως
ξυστραφέντες καὶ κοινῇ βουλευσάμενοι καταλύσουσι τὸν δῆμον).   Vischer,
ib. p. 171, "The opponents of democracy split into a number of
different clubs, which did not follow a common end, but each
their own advantage, now combining, now contending with each
other."

[6] Thuc. iii. 82, οὐ γὰρ μετὰ τῶν κειμένων νόμων ὠφελίας αἱ τοι-
αῦται ξύνοδοι, ἀλλὰ παρὰ τοὺς καθεστῶτας πλεονεξίᾳ.   The combination of hetaeries at Samos (τὸ ἑταιρικὸν) is called a ξυνωμοσία
Thuc. viii. 48.   Cf. the oligarchic oath in Aristotle Pol. 1310 a, 9,
(not especially referred to Athens), καὶ τῷ δήμῳ κακόνους ἔσομαι καὶ
βουλεύσω ὅ τι ἂν ἔχω κακόν.

in communication with one another[1], and with si- *clubs with*
milar clubs among the allies[2], by periodical meetings *one another*
of their leaders to decide on the course of action *and with*
demanded by circumstances.   In the political events *the allies.*
of the period common action on the part of the
oligarchs can often be traced, and for the purpose
of uniting and instructing the ordinary members of
the party this organization must have been of the
utmost service.

   With this network of combination the oligarchs *Hostility*
worked persistently against the constitution.   To this *of the oligarchs to*
end everything was subordinated[3], and their attitude *the con-*
on questions of ordinary politics generally depended *stitution.*
on a calculation of how their cause might be best
advanced.   Besides the method of direct attack on
the democracy, there was another method by which

   [1] There is little evidence for this.   Müller-Strübing (Der Staat
der Athener, Philologus, Supplementband, iv. pp. 71 ff.) argues
that it was usual for delegates to meet and discuss the policy to
be adopted.   He sees a probable allusion to this in Thuc. viii. 54,
and 48 (ὅπως μὴ στασιάσωσιν), where the warning against disunion
points to common action.
   [2] Cf. Thuc. viii. 48, where he refers to promises made to the
allies: this correspondence must have been secret.   Müller-Strübing
l. c. thinks that the delegates from the allies, who visited Athens at
the time of the great Dionysia, would confer with the Athenian
oligarchs.
   [3] There were natural reasons, why they should have been opposed to war (see ch. iv.), but it seems possible that on some occasions they were anxious that Athens should renew the war, in the
hope that the victory of Sparta might further their plans.   They
probably supported the Sicilian expedition; and Müller-Strübing,
ib. p. 86, sees in the invasion of Lacedaemonian territory (Thuc.
vi. 105), which led to the renewal of the war, a manœuvre of the
oligarchs in command of the Athenian forces.

ultimate success might be assured. This was by an
insidious interference in political life to employ their
influence in embarrassing the democratic government, in weakening and discrediting it, in depriving
it of its champions and alienating its supporters.
They were anarchists, not only striving to effect a
revolution, but secretly working against the public
peace and endeavouring to render all government
impossible until their end was attained.

With these objects they shrunk from no means,
however disloyal or unscrupulous, and were ready to
effect their purpose by a treacherous understanding
with the national enemy, or by a system of terrorism
in which assassination played a prominent part.

Their treachery to Athens and indeed to Greece,
in combining with Sparta, Boeotia and Persia, is
established by a long catalogue of crime, which
begins with the action of Isagoras in inviting Spartan
aid and is continued down to the alliance of the
oligarchs with Lysander in 405[1].

Revolu-
tion of
411.
During the war, unless we are to recognize a
deliberate plot against the democracy in the mutilation of the Hermae[2], their first direct attack on the

---

[1] For the different instances of oligarchic treachery, see Vischer,
ib. pp. 158—164. See also Resp. Ath. ii. 15. The author admits
the treacherous intentions of the oligarchs. If the Athenians lived
in an island, he says, they would be relieved of all fear, μηδέποτε
προδοθῆναι τὴν πόλιν ὑπ᾽ ὀλίγων μηδὲ πύλας ἀνοιχθῆναι μηδὲ πολεμίους ἐπεισπεσεῖν...νῦν μὲν γὰρ εἰ στασιάσαιεν, ἐλπίδα ἂν ἔχοντες
ἐν τοῖς πολεμίοις στασιάσειαν, ὡς κατὰ γῆν ἐπαξόμενοι.

[2] I have discussed one aspect of this event below, p. 90. Most
modern authorities regard it as the comparatively innocent act of
a band of drunken revellers: I think, however, that the evidence
of Andocides is too explicit and direct to be neglected, and that

constitution was in the oligarchic revolution of 411.
This, although carried out with due observance of
legal formalities[1], was only effected after the assassination of opponents had thrown Athens into a
state of hopeless panic. After they had obtained
power the oligarchs abolished all constitutional
government, ruled with violent illegality[2], and were
ready to surrender the city to Sparta, rather than
give up their power.

There is good evidence that treachery played *Treachery*
some part at Aegospotami[3], and the action of Ly- *in 405.*
sander in delaying to reduce Athens, and of Theramenes in protracting his embassy, can only be
explained on the theory of a secret understanding
between the Spartan general and the Athenian oligarchs, a theory fully borne out by Lysander's action
in helping to establish the government of the Thirty[4].

The means to which the oligarchs resorted were *Method*
no less criminal than the ends for which they worked: *of the*
they employed a system of terrorism to stifle oppo- *oligarchs.*

the act was the result of a deliberate plot, of which the purpose
now is not clear.

[1] This possibly, as Müller-Strübing (ib. p. 91) thinks, was a
concession to the moderate *doctrinaire* members of the party.

[2] Thuc. viii. 70, ἔνεμον κατὰ κράτος τὴν πόλιν. The government of the Thirty was worse, Xen. Hell. ii. 3. 21.

[3] For a discussion of this see Grote viii. p. 11. Vischer, ib. p.
199 and Scheibe, ib. pp. 21—2 accept the evidence as conclusive.

[4] There seems to have been an oligarchic plot, and if so,
Theramenes was probably concerned in it, for he played a leading
part, as soon as any definite steps were taken. It is extremely
hard to explain his action as entirely and loyally dictated by
patriotism, though Pöhlig (Jahrbuch für class. Phil., Suppl. ix.
pp. 284 ff.) endeavours to defend him. Lys. 13. 9 charges him with
deliberate treachery, but that statement is not unbiassed.

sition. Thucydides[1] describes how in 411 all opponents were removed at Athens, until the people was
panic stricken, and dared take no action. Similarly
the ground was cleared in 404 by the removal of
Cleophon[2], and by the conspiracy against the generals
and other officers who still opposed the peace[3].

*Covert
attacks
on the
democracy.* But it was not often possible for the oligarchs to
make an open attempt at revolution. From motives
of policy they were obliged to conceal their real purpose; until they could declare it, their best course
was to undermine democracy that it might fall the
more easily. This side of their action is really more
important than the other; their efforts here must
have been continuous, and from their subtlety difficult to discern. The Athenians were always ready to
scent oligarchic plots, sometimes perhaps groundlessly;
but we may be quite sure that the oligarchs took advantage of every crisis, combined with any party and
supported any proposal to embarrass and weaken the
democracy, by showing its weakness, inconstancy and
instability, and depriving it of its proper defenders[4].

To carry out this purpose effectively the oligarchs,
who took a leading part in any political intrigue,
had to conceal their convictions, and to play the part
of enthusiastic democrats.

---

[1] viii. 66.
[2] Lys. 13. 12, 30. 12—13. This must have been a judicial
murder.   [3] The conspiracy of Agoratus, Lys. 13.
[4] The action of the Whigs at the beginning of the reign of
James II. affords an exact parallel. Cf. Macaulay, History of
England, ch. 4. "The Whigs were a small and disheartened
minority. They therefore kept themselves as much as possible
out of sight, dropped their party name, abstained from obtruding
their peculiar opinions on a hostile audience, and steadily supported

Thucydides[1] says that at the beginning of the oligarchic movement at Athens in 411 people were astonished at some of the men who declared for oligarchy. He is probably thinking especially of Pisander, Charicles and others like them, who took a prominent part in the Hermae investigation. Having thus secured a reputation for democratic zeal they now took a leading place in the oligarchy. These men may have been mere political adventurers, on both occasions playing for their own hand, and throwing in their fortunes with democracy or oligarchy indifferently; but it is conceivable that they were all along agents of the oligarchy, pretending loyalty to democracy in order to overthrow it[2]. *Oligarchs disguised as democrats.*

To enter into detail, we may fairly assume that the oligarchs joined with the other extremists in bringing about the overthrow of Pericles, that they were among those who forced the command at Pylus on Cleon in the hope of being well rid of him, and that there was a leaven of oligarchic disloyalty in Cleon's mutinous hoplites at Amphipolis[3]. *Survey of their action.*

It is not so easy to estimate their part in the events of 415. It is best however to leave the crime itself out of consideration, and look only at the events resulting from it; and we can do this with less

every proposition tending to disturb the harmony which as yet subsisted between the Parliament and the Court."

[1] viii. 66, ἐνῆσαν γὰρ καὶ οὓς οὐκ ἄν ποτέ τις ᾤετο ἐς ὀλιγαρχίαν τραπέσθαι.

[2] There is certainly great difficulty in accepting this theory in the case of Pisander, who throughout Aristophanes is ridiculed as one of the war party. Though he may have really changed sides, there must have been many oligarchs in the disguise of democrats.　　　[3] Droysen, Hermes, ix. p. 16.

difficulty, because the most important consequence,
the banishment of Alcibiades, was not directly connected with the mutilation of the Hermae, but only
resulted from the state of panic into which the city
was thrown. It is impossible to suppose that the
oligarchs took no part in these proceedings. The
banishment of Alcibiades was ascribed to them by
Isocrates[1], and we know that Thessalus, who was probably an oligarch, drew up the information against
him. Besides this it is obvious how much they
gained by it. The state was enervated by the fever-
ish state of panic and suspicion that was kept up,
the civic body suffered the loss of many citizens who
were banished, and the democracy lost its ablest
leader in Alcibiades[2]. It cannot be denied that real
demagogues, such as Androcles, played an important
part, but it is probable that they were urged on by
oligarchs who used the mask of democratic sentiments to carry out their plans[3].

[1] Isocr. 16. 2 ff. This of course is not an impartial statement.

[2] Müller-Strübing, ib. pp. 81 ff., thinks that advantage was
taken of the state of affairs to endeavour to introduce the enemy.
Alcibiades was removed, the ναυτικὸς ὄχλος was far away in Sicily,
Athens was panic-stricken, and just then we hear of movements of
the Lacedaemonians and the Boeotians on the frontier. Thuc. vi.
61, Andoc. 1. 45.

[3] Götz (Jahrbuch für class. Phil., Suppl. viii. pp. 551 ff.) thinks
that Pisander, Charicles &c. were oligarchs at this time. He
traces the various informations to the intrigues of the oligarchs
and the counter moves of Alcibiades' friends. Thus the oligarchs
extended the scope of the enquiry to include Alcibiades. Hence
they procured the information of Andromachus ; this was answered
by the information of Teucrus which was called up by the ἑταιρεία
of Alcibiades. The attack of Androcles on Alcibiades was answered
by Alcibiades the Phegusian, who, evidently in the interest of his
namesake, suborned Dioclides.

They may also have contributed to the condemna-ion of the generals after Arginusae. Granting that the indignation aroused then was mainly natural and not factitious, it is probable that the oligarchs used their influence to foment the popular feeling and so bring about the downfall of the generals, who had done so much for the state and might do so much more.

We cannot trace the action of the oligarchs any further. Even in the conjectures which have been put forward we are on no sure ground, for it is impossible to obtain any certainty about a party whose workings were designedly secret. We can only infer that, as whenever they declare themselves in politics their action is treacherous and baneful, their veiled movements must have been no less hostile to the constitution.

Their organization could not have been main-tained in efficiency without constant exercise, and though the occasions were rare on which they decided on a plan of united action, the separate oligarchic clubs must have been constantly on the alert, and their indirect influence on politics was probably more important than their open attempts.

§ 3. *The Middle Party.*

In discussing the lines of party division in Athens, *A third political party.* I argued that besides the two extreme sections of oligarchs and democrats, there was a third political party to be taken into account. This party was composed of men of moderate views, who, though they might criticize the constitution, were not disloyal to

it, and formed the regular opposition to the democratic policy.   Their existence, although not brought
into prominence by our authorities, was, I thought,
sufficiently established by the history of the period.
On this account it demands the same discussion as
the other political sections; but in studying this
party we are not on such sure ground, and can only
deduce its character from the course of politics, and
from the views held by individual members of it.

No distinc-
tive title.   Modern historians have used different terms to
describe members of this party, such as "moderate
democrats," and "moderate oligarchs," and we are allowed this latitude because they do not seem to have
had a distinctive title[1].   If, however, we are to have a

---

[1] This is scarcely to be wondered at.   The historians assume a
general knowledge of politics, and do not explain the composition
of parties.   Thucydides occasionally mentions δῆμος and ὀλίγοι in
a political sense, but usually attributes the action of the state to
the Athenians as a whole, cf. ii. 59, iii. 36, 49, &c.   In iii. 41 he
does not mention the section to which Diodotus belongs, though he
has distinguished Cleon as ὁ τῷ δήμῳ πιθανώτατος.   With the
author of the Resp. Ath., every one who is not a χρηστὸς is a
πονηρὸς, and he draws no distinctions.   Still there are a few
traces of this party in history.   Thuc. iii. 82 talks of τὰ μέσα
τῶν πολιτῶν, after discussing the δῆμος and ὀλίγοι.   In viii. 75 he
talks of οἱ διὰ μέσου.   Similarly Euripides, Suppl. 244, talks of
the party ἡ 'ν μέσῳ.   Aristotle in discussing the μέσοι is thinking
of them more as a class than a political section, but he practically
assumes the identity.   These references justify the title of 'centre'
party; there are passages where they seem to be distinguished as
the 'moderates.'   Thus Alcibiades in his speech at Sparta (Thuc.
vi. 89) says that he and his family, while tolerating democracy,
tried to be μετριώτεροι τῆς παρούσης ἀκολασίας.   Thuc. iv. 28 calls
the opponents of Cleon οἱ σώφρονες.   This word seems to have
had a special political sense, as in viii. 53, εἰ μὴ πολιτεύσομέν τε
σωφρονέστερον, refers to the proposed reform of the constitution
in 411, and in 64, σωφροσύνη is used as equivalent to oligarchy.

denomination suitable to the party as a whole, I think the neutral title of "the middle party" is best, inasmuch as the **party** was united not so much by political sympathies as by the fact of **their** difference from both the extreme sections.

This party met with most favour from the middle *This party* class, who are generally in all states inclined to *mainly* *recruited* moderation in politics, and especially from the farmers *from the* *middle* of moderate property (Aristophanes' ideal character). *class.* The policy of the party as a whole was in the interests of the agricultural class, and on this account, as I have pointed **out above, must** have sometimes commanded the support of the small farmers, who wavered between this party and the democrats. The accession of this class probably gave them a majority in the assembly, for we find that on several occasions the middle party were in control of the government and able to carry their wishes into effect[1].

It is probable that the party was first organized *History of* under Nicias; it held together firmly during the first *the party* *during the* part of the war, and was able to carry its policy into *war.* effect in 421. During the years of peace the bonds of party discipline **were** relaxed; **the** policy of conciliation with Sparta, recommended by Nicias, was discredited **by the treacherous** conduct of that state, and the discredit reacted on the middle party. **As a** consequence the advocates of war returned to power, until the disaster at Mantinea once more restored the influence of Nicias. Soon after his party seems

The word **was** probably not a stereotyped political **designation,** but **was** used to point to **the** rash character of democracy. **Cf.** Diod. xiii. 53, οἱ ἐπιεικέστατοι.

[1] This is discussed below in chapter IV. p. 128.

to have broken up, as he was almost alone in opposing the Sicilian expedition [1].

Henceforth the middle party had neither a distinct policy of its own, nor indeed a separate existence, as its members attached themselves to one of
the other two parties. This result was natural; the
position of a middle party is at all times precarious,
but when politics become involved in passion and
violence, and the political issue is narrowed, it is
impossible to hold an even balance between the
extremes, and men must declare for one side or the
other [2].

At Athens this tendency was accelerated by economic changes brought about by the war. Agriculture was ruined; the richer landowners and farmers
of property were naturally opposed to war, and, as
time went on, joined the oligarchs in their desire at
all costs and by any means to overthrow the power
of the democrats and reverse their policy: on the
other hand the small peasant proprietors must have
gradually accustomed themselves to the conditions
of town life, and have joined forces with the democrats. From the year 410 we cannot trace the
existence of a middle party, but in the ranks of both
the democrats and the oligarchs we can distinguish
men of moderate political views.

*The middle party
and the
constitution.*

To discuss the middle party in detail, I propose
to consider first their attitude to the constitution,
and then their general policy. As we have seen, the

[1] Thuc. vi. 24, ἔρως ἐνέπεσε τοῖς πᾶσιν ὁμοίως ἐκπλεῦσαι. Cf.
Plut. Nic. 12.

[2] Possibly it is to this that Thucydides is referring in iii. 82
when he says, τὰ δὲ μέσα τῶν πολιτῶν ὑπ᾽ ἀμφοτέρων...διεφθείροντο.

party shaded off on the one hand to the democrats, on the other to the oligarchs. It included men of keen democratic feeling, who, however, must be ranked with this party as being in opposition to the democratic policy, as well as men who would have preferred a moderate form of oligarchy. But these, and indeed the bulk of the party, usually accepted the constitution as it was and worked loyally under it. They were opportunists[1] on this point, and so long as the constitution in existence was not guilty of flagrant excess, and ensured a general security, they were content. Hence they went with the stream, and acquiesced, in democracy, till the current of events set in the direction of oligarchy, when they made no attempt to resist the movement.

Many men, indeed, who usually acted with this party, desired to see a moderate oligarchy established, and the revolutions of 411 and 404 were both carried out with their help. They did not, however, take sufficient precautions to prevent oppression and secure moderation, and on both occasions they broke from the oligarchs, when they saw the character of their government.

As I have said, the party was not homogeneous, and so did not pursue one ideal of government: we can see, however, by their action, when placed in

Reforms desired by this party.

---

[1] See Beloch, Att. Pol. p. 13. Cf. Eur. Suppl. 244—5 (speaking of this party),

τριῶν δὲ μοιρῶν ἡ 'ν μέσῳ σώζει πόλεις,
κόσμον φυλάσσουσ' ὅντιν' ἂν τάξῃ πόλις.

Aristotle, Pol. 1296 a, 8, seems to refer to the opportunism of the μέσοι, ὅτι δ' ἡ μέση βελτίστη, φανερόν· μόνη γὰρ ἀστασίαστος.

power, what were the principles which commanded their united support. They desired a limitation of democracy in two particulars[1]. They wished (1) to ✗ limit the absolute power of the people, either by restricting the franchise, or by defining the powers of the assembly: (2) to abolish pay for state services (except in the army).

Limitation of the powers of the people. There is a necessary connection between these two reforms, for if the franchise were limited to men of a certain amount of property, they would be able to serve the state without requiring pay, while it was only the system of pay which enabled the demos to take part in some functions of government. In 412 there was a reaction against extreme democracy and in consequence the government passed to the moderates; it was probably owing to their influence that the powers of the assembly and council were limited by the institution of the πρόβουλοι, who were themselves men of the middle party[2]. In 411 those of the middle party who supported the oligarchic movement did so in the hope that a government based on a limited franchise would be introduced[3], and it

[1] I have omitted to discuss the objection that some individuals who may be ranked with this party (e.g. Socrates) had to the lot, but the question was more one for philosophers than for practical politicians; and the system does not seem to have caused any general dissatisfaction.

[2] So far as we can judge from the little we know of them; Hagnon and Sophocles (identified by many historians with the poet) were members.

[3] The proposal to entrust power to the Five Thousand in 411 was probably put in as a blind to attract the moderates, cf. Thuc. viii. 65, 67, 72. They laid great stress on making this element a reality, and their disappointment was the cause of the split, ib. 89, 92, 93.

was their disappointment in this respect that caused them to break with the extreme oligarchs. They were then able to overthrow the oligarchy and establish a government after their own heart, based on the two essential conditions of a limited franchise and the abolition of pay[1].

The same thing happened in 404; those of the middle party who supported the institution of the Thirty did so in the hope that they would establish a constitution on a sufficiently broad basis[2] while avoiding the blemishes of democracy. They were again disappointed, and Theramenes for a second time led the malcontents, but he was no match for the extreme oligarchs.

On questions of general policy this party formed, *The middle* at least for the first half of the war, the regular op- *party and* position. They were during all this time the peace *cratic* party[3], and though they were not ready like the oli- *policy.* garchs to accept peace at any price, and so to betray Athenian interests to Sparta, they were anxious to bring the war to a conclusion, so long as peace involved no loss of honour or empire. On this as on other subjects they took up a position intermediate between the two parties, set themselves against extreme tendencies in either direction, and became the

---

[1] Thuc. viii. 97.

[2] Thus Theramenes (who probably desired a more restricted franchise than most of the middle party), objected to the limit of 3000 being fixed, Xen. Hell. ii. 3, 19. His own ideal is expressed ib. ii. 3, 48; he was opposed to οἱ δοῦλοι καὶ οἱ δι' ἀπορίαν δραχμῆς ἂν ἀποδόμενοι τὴν πόλιν, being admitted to citizenship: on the other hand he objected to the tyranny of an absolute council.

[3] See chapter IV. p. 119.

advocates of compromise. On this account their policy always seems negative, and Nicias' attitude was one of monotonous opposition to the democratic proposals. In fact it would be possible to deny to this party any positive merits in statesmanship, were it not that it is redeemed by a few men, for whose proposals the party may claim credit.

Aristopha-nes a repre-sentative of the party.   Above all others Aristophanes may be regarded as the representative man of this party, and I think we can trace in his works a definite and consistent policy, which he constantly advocates[1]. He stood midway between the extreme democrats and the oligarchs; while severe on the faults of democracy and castigating the evil side of the assembly and of the law courts, and the system of state pay[2], he had no sympathy with the oligarchs[3], and was

---

[1] Aristophanes was a partisan, and, as I have argued above, his delineation of character did not always keep on truthful lines; but this did not hinder him from having genuine political ideas, and seriously advocating them. Th. Kock (Rhein. Mus. xxxix. pp. 118 ff.) insists on the serious purpose of Aristophanes. "The Aristophanic dramas," he says (p. 125), "are closely connected with the movements of popular feeling in politics and education, religion or art, with the practical aim of affecting the movements by conviction; they are distinctly didactic."

[2] The evils of the ἐκκλησία were the power of the demagogues and the abuse of ψηφίσματα. The evil side of the law courts was the system of συκοφαντία. Aristophanes' attacks on these and on μισθοφορά are too well known to require illustration. The Equites in particular is directed against demagogy, as impersonated in Cleon.

[3] This we may see in Lys. 577, where he attacks τοὺς συνιστα-μένους (a passage significant from the date at which the play was produced). He also attacks individual oligarchs, in cases where the motive of his attack seems political, Aves 126 (Aristocrates).

really loyal to the demos and eager for its prosperity[1].

The treatment of the allies advocated by Aris- *Party*
tophanes and other members of his party was in *politics and the*
accord at once with the highest statesmanship and *allies.*
humanity. I have argued that the allies suffered
few practical hardships from their subjection to
Athens, and that for this reason the demos in the
allied towns was really loyal, while the oligarchic
minority for selfish reasons was anxious for revolt.
So long, therefore, as Athens' power was unim-
paired, this connection was likely to be maintained,
but all the while the struggle between parties was
going on in all the states of the alliance; and the
decline of Athenian power and the growth of Spartan
influence in the Aegean strengthened the anti-
Athenian party and enabled them to carry out their
plans. The general revolt in 412 was due to the
feeling that Athens could not maintain the struggle
against Sparta for another year[2].

It was, therefore, in accordance with the deepest
interests of Athens to convince the allies that the
bond of union was not one of force and fear, but that
it was to their common interest to combine against
the common foe[3]. This the democrats did not see;
their policy was to maintain the alliance on the
existing basis, to assert their right to control the
allies, and to severely punish revolt: the oligarchs

[1] There is no trace of antidemocratic feeling in his works.
The Demos in the Equites is more sinned against than sinning.

[2] Thuc. viii. 2.

[3] This community of feeling was established with Samos
(Thuc. viii. 75), which remained faithful to Athens till the last.

7—2

on the other hand were working indirectly for the
dissolution of the alliance.   The best men of the
middle party seem, however, to have realized the
necessity of respecting the rights and feelings of the
allies, and of guarding against any unnecessary oppression.   This purpose we can trace in the speech
of Diodotus[1], as well as in the constant protests,
which Aristophanes raises against injustice to the
allies[2], and the appeals he makes for gentler treatment[3].

Proposals of Aristophanes for confederation.   Aristophanes, however, went further than this,
and advocated a scheme of "imperial federation,"
at a time when many of the allies were breaking off
their allegiance, and others were preparing for revolt.
In the passage of the Lysistrate (which was produced
in 411) where he is talking of the evil plight of the
state and the means of salvation, he laments the
isolation and disconnection of the allied states, and
proposes a union of allies, citizens, and aliens under
one great government[4].   It is scarcely possible to

---

[1] Thuc. iii. 42—8. The speech, whether authentic or not,
must have represented the views of many statesmen.

[2] The Babylonii was apparently written expressly to show up
the defects of the Athenian dominion, cf. Ach. 642. The oppression of the allies is referred to in Eq. 1070 (a protest against νῆες
ἀργυρολόγοι), ib. 802 (probably a reference to the φόρος), and Pax
639, 644.

[3] Eq. 1309, the opponent of Cleon is called ταῖς νήσοις ἐπίκουρε.
Pax 759, Aristophanes calls himself the champion of the allies.
ib. 935, he advocates a gentler treatment of them, ὥστ᾽ ἐσόμεθα
καὶ τοῖσι συμμάχοισι πρᾳότεροι πολύ.

[4] Lys. 582—6. The passage is worth quoting :

κaὶ νὴ Δία τάς γε πόλεις, ὁπόσαι τῆς γῆς τῆσδ᾽ εἰσὶν ἄποικοι,
διαγιγνώσκειν ὅτι ταῦθ᾽ ἡμῖν ὥσπερ τὰ κατάγματα κεῖται,

overestimate the significance of this passage. It contains a recognition of the weak spot in the Athenian empire, and proposes a remedy of the broadest statesmanship. It came too late, but to have formulated such a proposal is, in itself, a proof of deep political wisdom.

This feeling for Hellenic unity found expression *Feeling for Hellenic unity.* in other ways. Aristophanes, who is here at one with the rest of the middle party, was constant in his advocacy of peace[1] and alliance[2] with Sparta. Nicias and Laches were, in this respect, reviving the traditions of Cimon's policy[3], which was to maintain the friendship of Athens and Sparta, with mutual regard for each other's dominion. In 421 they seemed to have attained their goal; but the jealousy of the rival powers was too great for the settlement to last, the national party both in Athens and Sparta asserted itself, and the selfishness and bad faith of Sparta soon broke up the agreement.

The policy of union revived another principle of *Greece and Persia.* Cimon's policy, the principle of peace among the Greeks and war with Persia. It was obvious that the struggle between Athens and Sparta, which in

χωρὶς ἕκαστον· κᾆτ' ἀπὸ τούτων πάντων τὸ κάταγμα λαβόντας
δεῦρο ξυνάγειν καὶ συναθροίζειν εἰς ἕν, κᾆπειτα ποιῆσαι
τολύπην μεγάλην, κᾆτ' ἐκ ταύτης τῷ Δήμῳ χλαῖναν ὑφῆναι.

The δεῦρο ξυνάγειν καὶ συναθροίζειν εἰς ἕν can only refer to a common council of the alliance at Athens.

[1] Aristophanes wrote seven plays with the express purpose of advocating peace. (See Kock, ib. p. 119.)

[2] Cf. Pax 1080.

[3] See Beloch, Att. Pol. p. 48, Duncker, Griech. Gesch., Neue Folge, i. p. 91.

time brought all the Grecian states into conflict, could only result in weakening Greece to the advantage of Persia. That the war was for the benefit of Persia alone is abundantly evident from the effects of the peace of 404. Not only were the Ionian states surrendered to the enemy of Greece, but for a time all the states of Greece were simply vassals to the great king, and the supremacy of Persia only gave way to that of Macedon.

From the beginning of the war this prospect was manifest. Sparta was constantly sending embassies to Susa, Athens was not guiltless, and the degrading submission of both states to Tissaphernes, Pharnabazus and Cyrus in the latter part of the war was ominous enough.

Warning of Aristophanes. The danger must have been recognized by the more far-seeing Athenians, and operated as a powerful motive for peace. Peace, however, on terms which left the old state of rivalry and suspicion was not enough; there must be a real Panhellenic union, in which all the Greeks should give over their animosities and through mutual concession be united "by the elixir of friendship." Here too Aristophanes represents the best policy of his party, in constantly insisting on the folly of the civil war, on the danger of calling in Persia, and the glorious prospects which Panhellenism offered[1].

---

[1] He attacks embassies to the great king Ach. 62—130, 613, 647. Cf. Thuc. ii. 67, iv. 50. The danger from Persia is alluded to in Pax 108, where Trygaeus proposes to indict Zeus for betraying Greece to the Medes, cf. 408. He appeals to Panhellenic feeling in Pax 302,

ὦ Πανέλληνες βοηθήσωμεν εἴπερ πώποτε,

There is, therefore, much to praise in the policy advocated by Aristophanes, and inasmuch as he cannot have stood alone, and his views are in logical connection with the views of the middle party, we may credit that party with a leaven of the most exalted political ideas. *These ideas not realized by the middle party.*

But here their claim to admiration is exhausted. The exalted views of individuals did not obtain sufficient support to affect practical politics, and the party having no definite objects to pursue lacked solidarity. It is not enough to say that their actions fell short of their aspirations; so far as we can see, the practical statesmen of the party made no effort to realize their political ideas or to initiate a policy, except in the one particular of persistently advocating peace. They were fatally disposed to opportunism and compromise, they were content to wait upon events without energy to anticipate them.

The position of a party between two extremes is always difficult, and usually compels them to criticize and oppose, not to initiate and produce. The enthusiasm of carrying a consistent policy into effect belongs to the wings, the centre is cursed with barrenness.

where the Scholiast says μιᾷ προσηγορίᾳ αὐτοὺς περιέλαβε δηλῶν τὸ συγγενές. Ib. 996 he advocates a union of the Greeks,

μῖξον δ' ἡμᾶς τοὺς Ἕλληνας
πάλιν ἐξ ἀρχῆς φιλίας χυλῷ, κ.τ.λ.

When the danger had been realized in 411, he blames the Greeks. Lys. 433,

ἐχθρῶν παρόντων βαρβάρων στρατεύματι
Ἕλληνας ἄνδρας καὶ πόλεις ἀπόλλυτε.

CHAPTER IV.

PARTIES IN RELATION TO THE WAR. PARTY GOVERNMENT IN ATHENS.

The war the test question of politics. I HAVE reserved to the last the discussion of the war, so far as it divided parties at Athens. This is a subject which requires special consideration; for no other event possessed half the political importance of the war, which served for this period as the test question of politics. During the earlier years parties were almost equally divided on the subject, so that, although there was a constant state of warfare, there was usually a party advocating peace, now and again with success.

The interests of classes in the war. The relation of the different parties to the war depended on the interests of the classes composing those parties; this subject must accordingly be considered first. It is necessary for this purpose to look at the matter from two aspects. The interest of classes in the ultimate issue of the war and in the questions at stake is an entirely different question from the immediate profit or loss, which fell to their lot from the actual continuance of the war. With respect to the first point I have argued that it was in the interests of the democracy to continue the

war, until a balance of advantage had been attained,
and on this account the democratic party was resolved to carry it to a decisive conclusion. I shall
have to return to this point below: but for the
present I wish to discuss the immediate effects of
the war. It is obvious that in this connection we
must consider not only the wealth and poverty of
the different classes, but the source of their wealth
and their means of livelihood. The war had not the
same effect on agriculture and trade; but in the
long run, though different classes suffered in different
degrees, no class directly profited by it.

Some historians dismiss this question by a sweep- *Theory*
ing generalization. They assume that demagogues *that the*
and democrats alike found in the war a source of *war bene-*
profit, and that both in beginning and continuing it *lower*
they were actuated solely by self-interest. In the *classes.*
case of the demagogues the charges of Aristophanes[1]
are quoted and accepted[2] as conclusive proof, although there is no other evidence against them. It
is more important to discuss the interests of the
democratic party in general; and the case against
them is stated in an extravagant form by Freese[3].

" The rich men," he says, " desired peace in order *Freese's*
to be relieved of the trierarchy, the country people *theory.*
to leave their quarters in the town and return to
their fields: the industrial class desired peace, for
slaves were harder to manage and deserted: all

[1] Pericles Ach. 535, Pax 605. Pisander Babyl. fr. 81 (Kock),
Lys. 491. Cleon Eq. 801, 864, &c.

[2] E.g. by Hermann, Staatsalt. § 164.

[3] Der Parteikampf der Reichen und der Armen, p. 70, referring to the second part of the war.

whose income depended on the allies desired peace,
for the war was causing their revolt every day."
This is excellent as a description of the natural
interests all men had in a state of peace, and at first
sight seems to be intended for an enumeration of
the whole body of citizens in their several divisions.
We are led to wonder what was the obstacle to
peace; the explanation comes in the next line:
"Yet those who had nothing wanted war." We are
obliged to assume that the destitute poor were able
to carry their wishes into effect, against the combined strength of the rich, the middle class (admitted by the writer to form a majority), the country
people, the industrial class in the town, as well as
the indefinite class "whose income depended on the
allies." This in itself is a sufficient strain on our
credulity; it is worth while to see what reason he
assigns for the attitude of the poor. "They could
lose nothing by war, in which they found opportunity for service. The equipment of the fleet occupied them, service on it gave them pay[1]." Lastly
this has to be reconciled with a further proposition
of the same writer that "the citizen wished not to
work, but to live for the state and to be maintained
by it[2]." Surely he would have more chance of a
leisured existence in a time of peace, when he might
live presumably on the tribute coming in from the
allies[3], instead of earning his bread by fitting out

[1] Der Parteikampf, p. 16; the latter statement is hardly correct.

[2] Ib. p. 35.

[3] Perhaps *this* is the class "whose income depended on the
allies."

the fleet. On the theory that citizens were usually maintained out of the revenues of the state, we are obliged to assume that war made life not only less luxurious but more laborious[1]. I think it is evident that one theory destroys the other[2].

The main conclusion of this writer is at least *Effects of* in some degree generally accepted; it is necessary *the war.* therefore to examine the actual consequences of the war, and then to estimate the loss suffered by the different classes of the community. We may divide the results of the war into the loss in men, the loss in money, the effect on agriculture and trade, and the general discomfort produced by a continual state of war. It will be enough to summarize here the facts which are admitted, without discussing the evidence on which they are based.

Taking the population generally there was an *Decline of* almost continual decline[3]. At the beginning of the *popula-* war there were (not including the families of the *tion.* citizens and metoecs)

35,000 citizens, 10,000 metoecs, 100,000 slaves;

from the effects of the plague these numbers de-

---

[1] For this compare the aversion of the really idle and state-supported democracy of the fourth century to undertaking war.

[2] I have discussed the argument of Freese at some length, because it is based on theories commonly accepted by writers on the subject, but not generally stated so definitely as to admit of adequate criticism. Beloch, Att. Pol. p. 27, says, "The war became the basis for a new division of parties, in which it was above all the *personal interests of individuals* that determined their place in politics."

[3] I have taken the figures from Beloch, Bevölkerung, p. 99. The numbers are only approximate and proportional.

clined about 25 per cent, and there were 26,000
citizens, 7000 metoecs, 70,000 slaves. From 421
there was a slight improvement[1], which was however more than counterbalanced by the Sicilian
expedition and the Decelean war (the latter causing
the loss of a large number of slaves); and the numbers at the end of the war may have been about

20,000 citizens, 5,000 metoecs, 65,000 slaves.

Taking the military forces[2] separately, there were in
431 about 20,000 hoplites and cavalry, composed of
about 16,000 citizens and 4000 metoecs. By the
plague and war these numbers were reduced to
about 12,000 and 3000 respectively. After 412[3]
there were scarcely more than 9000 citizens, and
2000 metoecs of hoplite census, and at the end of the
war the citizen hoplites were about 8000.

Import-
ance of
finance to
Athens.
Finance was of scarcely less importance than
population. Athens could not put land forces in
the field with the same ease as Sparta, for most
of her allies had purchased immunity from service.
She required pay not only for her own soldiers,
but for mercenaries (especially for light-armed
troops and rowers employed on the fleet). The
fleet, in fact, entirely depended on the revenue;
the promise of higher pay induced the sailors to
change sides[4], and in the latter years of the war

[1] Thuc. vi. 12.

[2] Beloch, ib. p. 71. The number at the beginning of the war
may be open to dispute, but the losses are fairly well known.

[3] In the Sicilian expedition 2700 hoplites ἐκ καταλόγου, 1500
heavy-armed Thetes, 250 knights were employed, most of whom
perished. Beloch, ib. p. 67.

[4] Plut. Lysand. 4.

Athens was on this ground unable to maintain an efficient fleet[1]. The war resolved itself into a monetary contest, the sources of Athenian revenue were destroyed, and in spite of spasmodic efforts to raise money by booty and forced contributions, she was no match for the Persian subsidies, which were freely at Sparta's disposal.

Coming to details of finance, there was an enormous and permanent increase in the expenditure, which the increased revenue was not sufficient to meet. After a time the revenue declined, the most important sources were completely cut off, individual citizens were impoverished, and the reserves accumulated from surpluses in time of peace were exhausted. *Effect of the war.*

The annual revenue from ordinary sources at the beginning of the war is said to have been about 1000 talents[2], of which 600 came from the allies. In the course of the war, by the increase of tribute and other changes, it was raised to about 2000 talents[3]. From 413, owing to the occupation of Decelea and the revolt of the allies, it was enormously reduced. *Revenue.*

The ordinary expenditure of the peace establishment bore no relation to that required by the war. *Expenditure.*

---

[1] Thus Conon reduced his fleet from 100 to 70 ships because he could only man this number, Xen. Hell. i. 5. 20.

[2] Xen. Anab. vii. 1. 27.

[3] Arist. Vesp. 657. The increase of tribute would not account for the difference between this amount and that given by Xenophon, and as Aristophanes does not mention the εἰσφορά, we must assume that they are not reckoning the same items of revenue. Possibly Aristophanes is exaggerating, as his argument requires a large revenue.

The former is estimated by Böckh[1] at about 400 talents a year, an amount which other writers think unduly high.   It was, however, vastly below the revenue, as the large surpluses accumulated in peace testify.

From our knowledge of these surpluses and of the ordinary revenue, and from the general accounts of the treasury, which have been preserved in inscriptions, we are able to calculate the expenses of the war.   I summarize the results of the latest investigation[2].

Financial history of the war.   For the first nine years of the Archidamian war from 431/0 to 423/2 the funds employed for war purposes were approximately as follows:—

The loans from the temple treasures amounted to 5000 talents[3].   The receipts from the allies, at the rate of 600 talents for the first six years, and 1200 for the next three, amounted to 7200 talents; besides this a property tax (εἰσφορὰ) of 200 talents was raised for six years from 428/7, which brought in 1200 talents.   The other revenues would more than suffice for the ordinary expenses of administration.   This therefore gives us a total of more than 13,000 talents, or an average expenditure of 1500 talents a year on the war.

This expenditure had exhausted the treasury, and the war for the next two years had to be supported out of the ordinary revenues.   This may account for the remissness of the Athenians in Thrace, and must

---

[1] i. p. 320.

[2] Beloch, Rhein. Mus. xxxix. pp. 244—9.

[3] About 4150 talents from 431 to 427/6, and about 800 from then to 423/2.

have been a most urgent motive for concluding peace, though Thucydides does not mention it[1].

During the years of peace the finances naturally recovered, and we have it on fair authority[2] that 7000 talents were stored in the Acropolis. The loans from the temple began again in 415, and in consequence of the Sicilian expedition the treasury was emptied (with the exception of the reserve of 1000 talents)[3].

For the ten years from 422/1 to 413/2 we may reckon that more than 12,000 talents were spent on war purposes[4]. After this we have no accurate data of either revenue or expenditure, as the tribute was superseded by indirect taxation and the extent of the Athenian dominion varied. The reserve of 1000 talents was spent, a property tax was twice imposed, and extraordinary contributions were levied. We are reduced to speculation, and the average of 1100 talents[5] for the last seven years may not be far from the truth. This makes the total public expenditure on the war about 35,000 talents[6], without

---

[1] In v. 14 where he gives the Athenian motives.

[2] Andoc. 3. 8, which Beloch l.c. thinks exaggerated, as Athens had still to meet the cost of operations in Thrace, Melos and the Peloponnesus.

[3] Thuc. viii. 15.

[4] The tribute of the allies alone during that period would have produced this amount.

[5] This Beloch (ib. p. 249) thinks the minimum, as certain sums omitted from consideration above must be added (e.g. expenditure of 405/4).

[6] In the present value of money, according to Beloch, about £30,000,000. I have throughout accepted his figures without discussion, as for the purpose of the argument strict accuracy is not essential. It is probable, that he has, if anything, under-stated the expenditure, as he assumes that the φόρος alone of the

reckoning the expenditure of individuals (e.g. on the trierarchy), which we know to have been considerable.

Effect of the war on agriculture. The expenditure of the state on the war, enormous as it was, probably fell short of the losses suffered by individual citizens owing to the ruin of agriculture and the disturbance of trade. In the first years of the war it was part of the Spartan military plan to invade and ravage Attica, sweeping off her crops, and rendering agriculture almost impossible. The extent of the ravages varied with the duration of the invasion, but the effects in any case were disastrous. The capture of the Spartan prisoners at Sphacteria prevented invasion for a time; but the evils were intensified to an enormous extent by the occupation of Decelea[1], which made invasion permanent. Agriculture was out of the question, all agricultural property was lost, large numbers of slaves deserted, and almost the whole of the food supply had to be imported[2].

Corn supply. What this must have involved we may judge from the fact that in ordinary years 800,000 medimni of corn were imported[3], while Attica produced at the lowest estimate the same amount[4]. Athens, there-

ordinary revenue was employed for war purposes, while if Aristophanes (referred to above) is correct, there was an income of 2000 talents down to 412 against an expenditure for ordinary purposes of only 400.

[1] For the effects of this, see Thuc. vii. 27—8. 20,000 slaves deserted, the live-stock was lost (the cattle can scarcely have been seized by the Spartans, it seems likely that they were sent to Euboea).

[2] Ib. 28, τῶν τε πάντων ὁμοίως ἐπακτῶν ἐδεῖτο ἡ πόλις.

[3] Dem. Lept. 32.

[4] Böckh's estimate of the corn produced in Attica (i. pp.

fore, had to import at least double the ordinary
amount of corn, both in the earlier period of the war,
and after the occupation of Decelea, while in the
latter period the cost of transport must have risen
steadily[1].

On the decline of Athenian trade we have no
direct information. It is a natural and obvious inference that a long war, which involved so great a
loss of men and property, which ruined agriculture
and the agricultural classes and completely transformed the conditions of life, must have caused a
serious disturbance of trade. This conclusion is confirmed by a consideration of the nature of Athenian
commerce. It seems probable that under ordinary
circumstances the products and manufactures ex-
ported by Athens were inconsiderable in proportion
to her imports. Apart from the precious metals,
which were either found in Attica or contributed by
her allies, the deficiency must have been made good
by the important carrying trade with the rest of
Greece, which Athens enjoyed[2]. To maintain her

Conditions of Athenian trade.

97 ff.) is 2,400,000 medimni, a stupendous amount required by
his theory of population, and indeed the great argument against it.
But taking the lower estimate of population Attica would have to
produce at least as much as she imported. In 412, when population had declined and there were no cattle to feed, perhaps there
would not be so large an amount of corn required, but other food
must have been scarce and there must therefore have been a larger
consumption of corn per head.

[1] Thuc. vii. 28, ἥ τε τῶν ἐπιτηδείων παρακομιδὴ...περὶ Σούνιον
κατὰ θάλασσαν πολυτελὴς ἐγίγνετο.

[2] Gilbert, Handbuch, i. pp. 317—8. Böckh, i. pp. 75—6, lays
stress on the importance of this branch of trade, and the high
profits derived from it.

W.   8

position in this respect Athens required on the one hand the command of the sea, and on the other freedom of traffic with other nations.

Effect of the war on trade. To apply these considerations to the circumstances of the Peloponnesian war, Athenian merchants had to look forward from the first to the loss of their market in the Peloponnesus and in parts of Northern Greece. At the beginning of the war the building and equipment of the fleet and the increased importation of corn must have given a great impulse to trade in the Aegean. But the profit derived from this quarter cannot have afforded at all adequate compensation for the loss of trade in Greece. Moreover, the abnormal expenditure of the state and the direct taxation of the richer men diminished the available capital, and at the same time the increase of tribute reduced the purchasing power of the allies. This state of things continued until the peace of Nicias. During the following years much of the lost ground was doubtless recovered. But from 415 the decline of trade was constant. The Sicilian expedition had been regarded as a good investment for capital, and its failure involved the loss of all that had been invested. The revolt of the allies and therewith the loss of the chief Athenian market followed close upon this disaster, while the exertions of Athens' enemies at sea rendered her supremacy uncertain and contributed to the insecurity of trade. The final result of the war was for the time as ruinous to trade as it was to agriculture.

General distress Meanwhile there must have been a general rise of prices, and most of the poorer classes lost their

ordinary employment in trade or agriculture, while *and dis-comfort.*
the army chiefly and usually employed the men of
hoplite rank, and at a wage below that which was to
be gained industrially. We must also take into
account the removal of the farming class from the
country to the town. Men who were accustomed to
live in the fields were cramped in small, unhealthy
dwellings in a city which usually accommodated
only half their number. This state of discomfort
was partial in the first part of the war, but permanent in the Decelean war, though the decrease of
population and the large numbers employed on the
standing fleet must then have afforded some relief.

To recapitulate, while the successful conduct of *General effects of the war.*
the war depended on efficiency of troops and equip-
ment, and the issue came to depend on the possession
of the longest purse, the Athenians had to suffer a
decrease of population and of military forces, as well
as a decline in revenue, and an enormous increase
in expenditure. These losses were aggravated by a
total ruin of agriculture, a serious disturbance of
trade and a rise of prices, at a time when the people
had to endure all the dangers and discomforts of a
besieged city[1].

In these circumstances it is difficult to understand how any class can have profited positively by
the war, when the losses of all are so obvious.

The rich had most to lose, and they had to bear *Losses of the rich.*
the burdens of war. If their interests were com-
mercial, they suffered in the loss of trade; if on the

[1] These evils were only fully developed after 413, but none of
them (except the decline in revenue) were altogether absent in the
first part of the war.

8—2

other hand their property was in land, they must
have seen their country estates wasted and destroyed[1].
They had to contribute the greater share of the property tax, which for some time was regularly imposed,
and the trierarchy was a permanent and exhausting
burden. The loss they suffered is attested by the
institution of a divided trierarchy in the latter years
of the war[2], as well as by the impoverishment of
formerly rich families[3].

Losses of the middle class. The middle class were, for the most part, engaged
in agriculture, and therefore suffered the most direct
loss. The richer members had to contribute to the
property tax, and to undertake the hoplite service
at pay that was not fair remuneration for them.
The small farmer was ruined by the break up of
agriculture, while he was unfitted and indisposed for
a town life with the discomfort it involved.

Sufferings of the poor. Lastly the poor without land or capital were not
exempt. Although from the fact that they could
not lose much, they recovered more quickly from
the effects of war, they were the first to feel the pinch
of poverty[4]. The rise of the prices of necessaries
affected them more keenly than it did other classes,
and at the same time they had not the same opportunities of earning their living, owing to the decline

---

[1] Cf. Pericles' speech, Thuc. ii. 62, and ib. 65, οἱ δὲ δυνατοὶ
καλὰ κτήματα...ἀπολωλεκότες, κ.τ.λ.

[2] Isocr. 18. 59. See Gilbert, Handbuch, i. p. 351.

[3] Lys. 19. 47, 26. 22. Xen. Mem. ii. 8. 1. See also Beloch,
Att. Pol. p. 6.

[4] We have positive testimony of their suffering from the war ὁ
μὲν δῆμος ὅτι ἀπ' ἐλασσόνων ὁρμώμενος ἐστέρητο καὶ τούτων, Thuc. ii.
65.

of trade and the increased competition[1]. To them, too, the loss of their ordinary pleasures and the state of discomfort in which they had to live must have forcibly appealed.

I think we are justified in concluding that there was no class to which the war in itself appeared advantageous, and that in the constant support of the war during this period men were actuated by political convictions, and not by personal interests. *Parties divided by political convictions.*

A consideration of the objects for which the war was waged, and of the great questions involved in it, will show on what basis these convictions rested. The war was undertaken by Sparta with the intention of breaking up the Athenian alliance and reducing Athens from the position of a great power. As the war went on still greater things were at stake. Down to the peace of Nicias, Athens was on the defensive; that convention settled none of the questions in dispute[2], and practically restored the state of affairs which had formerly rendered war inevitable and now made its renewal almost certain. After this had actually taken place, the situation was entirely altered by the Sicilian disaster, and the Athenians, who had fatally over-estimated the probability of success, saw themselves with largely diminished forces compelled to meet the alliance of *Questions at stake in the war*

[1] Beloch, Att. Pol. p. 27, thinks that the people of the town found their gain in the congregation of the country people in Athens, while the latter were reconciled to the loss of their farms by maintenance at state cost. The theory of state compensation I have discussed above. The advantage to the former class would be neutralized by the rise of prices and the increased competition.

[2] See Vischer, Kleine Schriften, i. p. 94.

Sparta, Persia and Syracuse. The war then became a struggle for Athens' existence as an independent state[1], and from the magnitude of the question at issue, as her prospects of victory declined, her resolution to resist to the last became firmer. In this contest Athens was fighting the battle of Greece, for Persia was on the other side, striving to reassert her old dominion.

War supported by the democrats. The objects at stake in the war were, in themselves, sufficient to decide the democrats in favour of a vigorous resistance, even without the reflection that concession to Sparta might endanger the democratic constitution[2]. These considerations induced many men, whose personal interests separated them from the bulk of the democratic party, to give a vigorous support to its policy. There was also a strong military party who, though not properly politicians, saw clearly enough that Athens' best interests were threatened by Sparta, and who were therefore enthusiastic for the war.

Military party. To this class generals like Lamachus and Demosthenes belonged, men who took no part in political life, but devoted their services loyally to a vigorous prosecution of the war. Such men were the trierarchs at Samos, who gave the first check to the oligarchic movement in 411[3], or the generals and

---

[1] Vischer, ib. p. 95, says, "In the Archidamian war the struggle was more for the maintenance or loss of the Athenian hegemony, than for the subjugation of one state by the other. In the second war Athens is fighting more for existence than sovereignty, and the war became for her one of desperation."

[2] See above, p. 34.

[3] Thuc. viii. 73.

taxiarchs, who offered so obstinate a resistance to
peace, even after Aegospotami, and had to be
treacherously removed by the oligarchs[1]. " The
twenty-seven years of the war," says Droysen[2], " show
on the part of Athens an obstinacy of resistance and
a versatility always ready to meet the growing power
and passion of the foe with well ordered strength
only possible under a firmly established military
organization."

On the other hand the oligarchs were not en- *Other*
thusiastic for the empire or the constitution, and were *parties and the war.*
prepared to sacrifice both to the enemy. As rich
men, whose property was largely invested in agriculture, they wished to be rid of the burdens and
losses of war, and were always ready to accept peace
on moderate terms, and sometimes on no terms at
all. But the oligarchs from their small numbers and
neglect of ordinary political methods were not so important representatives of the peace policy as the
middle party. This body, composed for the most
part of the middle class, were not so keenly interested
in the war as the democrats, while they suffered
more directly than any other class in the destruction
of agriculture[3]. Consequently in the first years of

---

[1] Lys. 13.

[2] Hermes, ix. p. 15.

[3] This appears in the plays of Aristophanes, who so constantly
contrasts the delights of peace with the evils of war. His hero is
usually the honest farmer of moderate property, cf. Ach. and Pax
passim and Menander fr. 719 (Kock),

$$\epsilon\iota\rho\eta\nu\eta \ \gamma\epsilon\omega\rho\gamma\grave{o}\nu \ \kappa\grave{a}\nu \ \pi\acute{\epsilon}\tau\rho\alpha\iota s$$
$$\tau\rho\acute{\epsilon}\phi\epsilon\iota \ \kappa\alpha\lambda\hat{\omega}s\cdot \ \pi\acute{o}\lambda\epsilon\mu\sigma s \ \delta\grave{\epsilon} \ \kappa\grave{a}\nu \ \pi\epsilon\delta\acute{\iota}\psi \ \kappa\alpha\kappa\hat{\omega}s.$$

See also Resp. Ath. ii. 14, Ar. Eccles. 197 ff.

the war they formed the constant advocates of peace ; but in the Decelean war their influence does not seem to have been so keenly exercised in this direction, probably because they saw that good terms could not be obtained.

Lastly there must have been a large body of men who, though not permanently attached to any party and in no constant relation to the war, shaped their action according to events, ready to carry on the war in prosperity and in distress anxious for peace. As neither the war party nor the peace party could of themselves command an absolute majority[1] (in the Archidamian war at least), this shifting section held the balance between them. If we are to decide to what class this section belonged, I think it would be safest to identify it with the peasant farmers of small property, who felt both the advantages for which the war was waged, and the evils which accompanied it. By the transfer of their support, they were probably responsible for the peace negotiations initiated by Athens, when the war was going ill, as well as for the rejection of the proposals of Sparta, when the fortunes of Athens were in the ascendant[2]. In the later course of the war, they had by the loss of their property become absorbed in the democratic party,

[1] This is evident from the course of events. See below, p. 128. See also Beloch, Att. Pol. 28.

[2] Ar. Pax 211—9, refers to the rejection of peace proposals by the victors, whenever any success was gained on either side. To the action of this class, we may ascribe the vacillation of policy, which Thucydides regards as characteristic of democracy. In three passages, where he describes a reaction of feeling or a change of policy, Thucydides uses the phrase ὅπερ φιλεῖ δῆμος, ὄχλος or ὅμιλος ποιεῖν (ii. 65, iv. 28, viii. 1).

and hence were more constant supporters of the war policy.

The test-question of party division was for the *War as a party question.* time not oligarchy and democracy, but peace and war. The opposition between the advocates of the rival policies appears first in the debate about the admission of Corcyra to the Athenian alliance, when, as Thucydides tells us[1], on the first day the Athenians approved the Corinthian arguments, but in the next assembly decided to support the Corcyraeans. This critical decision was only taken after a close party struggle, which was maintained throughout the first stages of the war. The representatives of the rival policies renewed the contest again and again with alternating success, and we are able to trace during this period the variations of party government, and their effects on politics.

It is always dangerous to compare ancient politics *Party government at Athens.* to modern, because in the former the government of the people was direct and not representative; but I think the contest of parties in Athens for political power justifies us in talking of party government.

We have seen that the two elements in the con- *Importance of the election of generals.* stitution entrusted with real power were the popular assembly and the board of generals. Now a party, which had a majority on the latter and could command the support of the former, was in practical control of the government. But the generals were elected by the assembly[2], and accordingly the party predominating on the board of generals must have had

---

[1] Thuc. i. 44.

[2] The assembly elected the generals, whether it voted in a body or κατὰ φυλάς. See note on next page.

the support of the people at the time of the election, and retained it until events brought their opponents into favour. Even then the generals had a certain degree of power, until their year of office expired, for they had the control of military operations, and their rivals could not take the initiative. As therefore the generalship was the most important office, election to it was keenly contested, and when a choice had to be made between alternative policies, the result of this election must have been for the time decisive[1].

[1] There are some minor points in connection with the election of the generals which I have left out of consideration.

1. The time of election has been much disputed. There is now a strong balance of opinion that the generals were chosen towards the end of Munychion (April) and entered on office in Hecatombaeon (July); see Beloch, Att. Pol. pp. 265 ff.; he discusses the question at length and quotes other authorities. If this date is correct there was an interval of about three months between election and entry on office, so that generals might hold office for three months after their policy had been condemned by the election of their opponents.

2. The method of election is quite unknown and there is the widest diversity of opinion. See Beloch, Att. Pol. pp. 276 ff. Gilbert, Beiträge, pp. 16—24, Droysen, Hermes ix. pp. 1 ff.—The two latter writers think that the generals were elected by the whole people, but that in the election regard was had to the tribes as far as possible, in order that each tribe might usually but not without exception be represented on the board. Beloch thinks that the πρύτανις was elected by the whole people from any tribe, but his nine colleagues by the separate tribes, one tribe losing by lot or rotation its right of election. This would answer to the facts well enough, as we occasionally find two generals elected from the same tribe, but the other eight are always, so far as we know, from eight other tribes. The subject is too obscure for a certain decision. There is one consideration pertinent to the political aspect of the strategia. If each general was elected ἐξ ἁπάντων (Poll. viii. 87) and by all, it would naturally result that one party having a majority of votes, would carry all the ten candidates. This is

If then we know the generals of any year, and *Lists of* the policy advocated by the majority, we have a clue *generals.* to the state of parties at the time, and can discover which of them was in control of the government. We are seldom able to obtain a full list for any year. We have usually to depend on the chance mention of three or four names in Thucydides and Xenophon, occasionally supplemented by information derived from inscriptions relating to the financial business and military operations of the year. These sources, however, usually contain enough to enable us to trace the transfer of power in successive years. The lists, so far as we know them, have been drawn up[1], and justify us in concluding that on most occasions the election of the generals was a political conflict of great importance, in which the parties put forth their utmost efforts.

The constant changes of policy and magistrates *False* which we see represented in this way throw a clear *theory of Athenian* light on the politics of the period, and enable us to *politics.* dispose of some fallacious theories which have hitherto been accepted. Of these the most important is, that, whatever may have been the strength of the different parties, the democracy alone took any important part in politics. Some trace this to the

clearly disproved by the lists of generals, for in years when political feeling ran high, we find men of opposite parties elected, e.g. Nicias and Lysicles, rival party leaders, in 428/7, so Nicias and Cleon in 424/3. The minority must have had some means of obtaining representation.

[1] By Beloch, Att. Pol., Anhang i. pp. **289** ff., where he gives a list of generals with a commentary quoting the authorities on which the list for each year is based. See also Gilbert, Beiträge, who discusses the generals elected each year.

terrorism established by the demagogues[1], others to
the want of a representative system[2]. The first explanation scarcely requires consideration, the second
is worth discussing. Every decision of the assembly
is regarded as the voice of the mob ; when a change
of policy occurs, it is traced to the fickleness of the
popular will, because, it is argued, the respectable
citizens did not as a rule attend the assembly, and
their voice was not heard owing to the lack of representation. We are told[3] that "the size of Attica
rendered the difficulty of attending the assembly so
great that those who lived at a distance did not
usually attend, and political power was in the hands
of the proletariate. It was really the inhabitants of
the town and Piraeus who filled the assemblies, passed
decrees, made laws, elected and deposed magistrates."
This may be true of the ordinary work of administration, at which no one was very anxious to attend[4];
but we cannot suppose that the middle class let everything go by default. It is reasonable to conclude
that the country people flocked in[5] to vote on any
great question (such as proposals for war or peace), as

[1] e. g. Curtius, vol. iii. p. 115 (English Trans.). His argument
is discussed and disproved by Müller-Strübing, Aristophanes, pp.
49—67, and Oncken, Athen und Hellas, ii. pp. 212 ff.

[2] The complaint is frequent. See Beloch, Att. Pol. p. 7,
(although his statement there is general, and does not refer to
the fifth century in particular).

[3] Beloch, l.c.

[4] Cf. Ar. Ach. 19, which shows the reluctance of citizens
to attend the ἐκκλησία.

[5] Even the obstacle of distance did not exist for the greater
part of the war, for the whole of the citizens were resident within
the walls, and had equal facilities of attending the ἐκκλησία.

well as at the annual elections.   Apart from the in-
herent improbability of one class, and that a minority,
controlling policy and legislation, we have direct and
positive evidence in the elections of generals and
the changes of policy, to show that government did
actually change hands, and was shared almost equally
between the war and peace parties.   Moreover at
debates in the assembly of which we have any de-
tailed account, both sides are usually represented,
and often with nearly equal votes[1].

The conflict of parties, the alternate triumph of *Summary*
different policies, and the general attitude of the *of political*
state to the war, can be best illustrated by an out- *history.*
line of political events, as concrete facts are so much
more convincing in this case than general conclusions.   In drawing up this outline I have only given
a bare record of the most important events, without
describing circumstances which qualified their general
tendencies; but for the purpose in view, the election
of generals each year, and the success or defeat of
the war and peace parties are sufficient.   As the
names of the generals are not completely known,
and many individual generals are men of no political
importance, I have usually only given the name of
the chief general, whose party was in power, the
party to which he belonged, their action on the
subject of war and peace, and other political events
of primary importance[2].

[1] Thuc. i. 44. See above p. 121; cf. iii. 49 (the debate on Mity-
lene) ἐγένοντο ἐν τῇ χειροτονίᾳ ἀγχώμαλοι, Xen. Hell. i. 7. 34.

[2] In the summary of Athenian policy, which follows, I have
consulted Beloch, Att. Pol., and Gilbert, Beiträge *passim*.   I have
not thought it necessary to quote the original authorities.

OUTLINE OF THE POLITICAL HISTORY OF ATHENS FROM 431 TO 404 WITH ESPECIAL REFERENCE TO THE ELECTION OF GENERALS AND THE QUESTION OF WAR AND PEACE.

Year	Generals in Power	Party in power	Actual policy on peace or war	Other political events, &c.
431/0	Pericles	War	War conducted on Pericles' Plan	Combination of extreme Democrats (under Cleon) and the richer class against Pericles
430/29	Opponents of Pericles	Peace	Peace embassy to Sparta unsuccessful. War mismanaged	Pericles probably rejected at the election of 430
429/8	Pericles	War		Pericles is restored to power and dies in the autumn of 429. Parties now nearly equal.
428/7	Nicias	Peace	Lesbos revolts. Financial difficulty, imposition of εἰσφορά	Death of Lysicles. Cleon succeeds to the προστασία
427/6	Nicias, Laches,&c.	Peace	Nicias inactive. Peace proposals of Athens rejected by Sparta	Relative power of the different parties seen in the debate about Mytilene
426/5	Hippocrates	War	War mismanaged	
425/4	Nicias	Peace	Blockade of Pylus. Cleon's victory there. Repeated peace embassies from Sparta	The success of Cleon brings the war party into power. Cleon's influence supreme. Raising of tribute and of dicast's fee
424/3	Cleon	War	War party discredited by the defeat at Delium and events in Thrace. Armistice concluded	Both parties (Cleon and Nicias) represented on the board of generals this year. The failure of the war policy produces an inclination to peace
423/2	Nicias (probably)	Peace	Conduct of Brasidas prevents conclusion of peace	Generals of this year entirely unknown. Nicias was probably elected
422/1	Cleon	War	The war party makes a last effort to recover Amphipolis. Cleon's defeat and death puts Nicias in power, and peace is concluded	Complete reversal of policy after Cleon's death. Nicias and Laches carry out their peace policy and conclude an alliance with Sparta
421/0 420/19	Nicias Alcibiades	Peace War	Alliance with Argos, resulting in indirect renewal of war with Sparta	Hyperbolus and Alcibiades succeed to leadership of war party
419/8	Alcibiades	War	Declaration on Athens' part that Sparta has broken the truce. Growing ill-feeling between Athens and Sparta	

Date	Leader		Event	
418/7	Nicias	Peace	In spite of the peace party being in power, the Athenians (through Alcibiades' influence) take part in the battle of Mantinea	The conflict between Nicias and Alcibiades, and the consequent vacillation of policy, lead to the resort to ostracism, in the spring of 417 (probably), which however only results in the banishment of Hyperbolus
417/6	Nicias	Peace	War with Sparta suspended owing to the Sicilian expedition	Alcibiades had joined forces with Nicias, and secured election to the generalship, but Nicias controlled the policy
416/5	Alcibiades			
415/4	Alcibiades			Fall of Alcibiades in the excitement raised by the mutilation of the Hermae. Combination of extremists against him
414/3	Extreme democrats	War	The descents of the Athenians on the Lacedaemonian coast lead to a declaration of war by Sparta, as Athens refuses arbitration. Decelea occupied (in spring of 413)	
413/2	Extreme democrats	War	Sicilian disaster. Revolt of allies	Extreme democracy discredited. The appointment of πρόβουλοι to manage the government. Henceforth the middle party are resolved on war
412/1	Moderates	War		Oligarchic conspiracy
411 Marchto July	Oligarchy	Peace	Three peace embassies to Sparta	
411/0	Moderates	War	Spartan peace proposals after Cyzicus rejected	Moderate democracy established on the overthrow of the oligarchy
410/9	Thrasylus	War		Full democracy restored. Moderate and extreme democrats coalesce
409/8 to 407/6	Alcibiades	War	Supposed peace embassy from Sparta in 408 (?)	Fall of Alcibiades in 406
406/5	Thrasylus	War	Peace embassy from Sparta after Arginusae. Proposals rejected by Athens	Trial of generals
405/4	Conon, &c.	War	Defeat at Aegospotami, probably due to treachery of Oligarchs. Spartan peace proposals rejected and resisted to the last. Unconditional submission to famine and treachery	

Conclusion to be derived from these facts. Such a map of political events enables us to realize vividly the energy and persistency with which the struggle of parties was kept up in Athens. The constant changes of government and of policy are sufficient proof that parties were sharply divided and equally resolute in the pursuit of their political ends. We may, therefore, reject the theory that the mob of the town had any monopoly of political activity. A brief review of the different periods of the war will show this more clearly.

Different periods of the war. The war falls naturally into three parts, the first[1] period going down to the peace of Nicias, the second[2] covering the years of peace, and the third[3] lasting from the renewal of the war to the surrender of Athens. Each of these periods has distinct characteristics; the struggle of the rival parties varied greatly in the first and last years of the war, and in the second period, which was one of nominal peace, the situation was complicated by the prominence of political questions other than those of war and peace.

Party struggles in the first part of the war. In the first years of the war parties were fairly matched and had an equal share of office. The advocates of peace and war controlled the government in turn, and each party endeavoured to use their influence in the assembly to carry their policy into effect. The changes of government were largely due to the course of events and the temporary success or failure of the rival parties. Thus the sufferings caused by the second invasion in 430 and the losses of Athens in 428–7 led to peace negotiations being

[1] 431—421.   [2] 421—413.   [3] 413—404.

opened in those years[1]. Similarly the success of
Brasidas in 424 induced the Athenians to consent to
an armistice, and the peace of Nicias was rendered
possible by the defeat of Cleon. There were, therefore, at least four occasions on which the peace party
took definite steps to realize their policy, while the
war party, profiting by their own good fortune or the
blunders of their opponents, procured the rejection
of Spartan proposals in several instances[2]. Generally
speaking a change of government was followed by a
change of policy; but on other occasions the peace
party were entrusted with office owing to the failure
of their opponents to conduct the war successfully,
and they were expected to continue military operations until the state had a favourable opportunity
for concluding peace[3].

During the years succeeding the peace of Nicias *Party*
the political situation was changed. The peace was *struggles from* 421
nominally preserved until 413, and in this interval, *to* 413.
as compared with the previous period, the position of
parties was inverted; the peace party endeavoured
to maintain the existing situation, and the war party
to disturb it. The government was again shared
between the two parties, and for the first few years
neither party had a decisive superiority, so that the
policy of the state was marked by vacillation and

[1] For the peace negotiations of 430 see Thuc. ii. 59. The
peace proposals mentioned in Thuc. iv. 21 and Ar. Ach. 653—4
are generally referred to the year 427; see Beloch, Att. Pol. p. 34.

[2] After Pylus the Spartans sent embassies on several occasions
in vain; Ar. Pax 665—7 evidently refers to these.

[3] Apparently in 428 and 425, although the peace party were in
power, they were not allowed to initiate peace negotiations.

W.   9

compromise. The history of the period is so involved
that it is worth while to review it briefly in detail.

The advocates of peace did not retain their position for long; a reaction of popular feeling brought
Alcibiades into power, and he was able to bring about
the alliance with Argos, which led Athens into indirect hostilities with Sparta[1]. This unsatisfactory
state of affairs, in which Athens was attacking a
power with whom she was nominally allied, reached
a climax in the battle of Mantinea. Nicias, who was
in office, was able to prevent any effective force being
sent against Sparta, while Alcibiades, who accompanied the expedition, managed to involve the
Athenian arms. This intolerable balance of power
caused the resort to ostracism in 417[2]. The rival
leaders agreed to submit their claims to the decision
of the whole state with some hope that for the future
the policy of one or the other might be carried out
vigorously and consistently. The intervention of
Hyperbolus led to a change of plan and to the combination of the former rivals. For the time Nicias
seems to have gained ground and Alcibiades took a
less prominent position[3]. In order to recover the
influence he had lost he advocated the Sicilian ex-

[1] Alcibiades could not get either the peace or alliance with
Sparta renounced by Athens; but he procured a formal declar-
ation that Sparta had broken the truce, Thuc. v. 56.

[2] The ostracism of Hyperbolus took place in some year between 418 and 415; on the whole there is more authority for
the date 417, and I have adopted Beloch's explanation of the
events connected with the ostracism (Att. Pol. pp. 54—5).

[3] Although both were generals, the policy of Nicias was carried
out; see Beloch, ib. p. 57.

pedition, and during his exile and the absence of Nicias Androcles and the extreme democrats brought about a renewal of the war.

After the disaster in Sicily there was no longer *Party* an even division of parties, and, except for the in- *till the* terval of the oligarchic revolution, the war was *end of* always vigorously supported by the government[1]. *the war.* The preponderance of the war party was due to two causes, which I have discussed above. On the one hand the social changes brought about by a long-continued war had altered the composition and relative strength of the different parties[2], and on the other the Athenians realized the importance of the war to Athens and to Greece, and were obsti- nately determined not to give way[3]. During the oligarchy of 411 three embassies were sent to Sparta, but with this exception the policy of resistance to the last was invariably maintained. The Spartan proposals were rejected whenever they were offered[4], and even after the crushing and hopeless defeat of Aegospotami the spirit of the Athenians was not broken, they refused every suggestion of concession and only yielded to the inevitable necessities of famine.

[1] The peace party, although in a minority, was not extinct. Its existence may be traced in Diod. xiii. 53, where he says that some Athenians advocated the acceptance of the Spartan propo- sals after Cyzicus.

[2] See above, p. 94.

[3] See above, p. 118.

[4] In 413 (Thuc. vii. 18), 410 (Diod. xiii. 53), 408 (See Gilbert, Beiträge, pp. 361—2), 406 (Schol. to Ar. Ran. 1533), 405. The proposals of 408 and 406 do not rest on good authority and are open to doubt; see Grote viii. p. 1 for the latter.

Final conclusions. Finally this survey of political events strengthens three important conclusions which I have already accepted on somewhat insufficient evidence. In the first place we may conclude that the conditions of political life at Athens were normal, that there was a balance of political forces which practically resulted in party government. There were regular principles of party division; parties were distinctly and not unequally divided, and they sought to obtain official power in order to carry their principles into effect. In the second place the great cause of party division was not the preference which men had for particular constitutional forms, but the one great political question which overshadowed all others. During the whole war, except for an interval of four months, the democratic constitution was maintained, almost without modification[1]; but the contest about war and peace was never suspended, the advocates of the rival policies were always confronting each other, and enjoyed in turn success or failure. Lastly the resolution of the Athenians to make no terms with Sparta rose, as their prospects of victory became more distant[2] and as their losses and sufferings were

[1] Reforms limiting the powers of the democracy were introduced in 413 (see above p. 96), and after the overthrow of the oligarchy full democracy was not immediately restored (see p. 97); but these modifications were due to exceptional circumstances and were merely temporary.

[2] The two critical disasters in the latter part of the war were the defeats in Sicily and at Aegospotami. After the first ἐδόκει χρῆναι μὴ ἐνδιδόναι (Thuc. viii. 1); and after the second the Athenians immediately prepared for a siege, and as time went on in spite of famine οὐ διελέγοντο περὶ διαλλαγῆς (Xen. Hell. ii. 2. 4 and ii. 2. 11).

every day aggravated. We may therefore conclude
that the general determination of a majority of the
citizens to carry the struggle to a decisive end was
founded not on a calculation of personal interest but
on political convictions. It was recognized that the
power of Athens and her dominion over other states,
even her independent existence, depended on a successful issue of the war. It is the merit of the democratic party that from the first they realized the
tremendous interests involved in the war and never
swerved in their resolve to defend those interests
without concession. And they must not be condemned for the result; the duel for the supremacy
between Athens and Sparta was a life and death
struggle, and it was impossible for Athens, at least,
to draw back.

"The Peloponnesian war was begun by Sparta
under vain pretexts and with guilty conscience; but
the Athenians themselves do not deny that for years
before they had gathered all their forces together and
braced themselves for a decisive contest. And the
moral responsibility for the war, in which this glorious nation consumed itself, Athens must bear. She
can bear the burden, for national unity is a treasure
on which a nation may stake its existence, and for
the sake of the Hellenes it was the duty of Athens
to fight the Dorians to the death. It was, therefore,
no vulgar ambition, no purposeless beating of the air,
when Athens undertook and carried on this war with
all her forces and with unexampled self-sacrifice; and
he who understands this will admire the Athenians
more in misfortune than prosperity.

"We do not quarrel with history. The doom of Athens was inevitable and not undeserved. But yet it was the conquered cause that pleased the gods; and we, mortals of a later day, cannot reflect without regret on the fall of this wondrous nation, which nature meant for the political ideal—but nature missed the mark[1]."

---

[1] This passage is adapted from the concluding words of Wilamowitz's Festrede "Von des attischen Reiches Herrlichkeit" (Aus Kydathen, pp. 44—5). He lays more stress on the claim of Athens to dominion over the other Greeks than I have done; but the passage seems on the whole so true that it may fairly be quoted in support of my argument.

INDEX.

References in all cases are to Athenian politics and institutions.

Phrynichus, work on the Athenian
Constitution ascribed to, 8 n. 2

Pisander, as a demagogue, 61; possibly a disguised oligarch, 90,
n. 3

Plutarch and Athenian history, 10

Political Parties, uncertainty and
difference of opinion on, 12; divided by political principles, 35;
divided by questions of the day,
36; three in number, 38; composition of, 39, 45; struggle of,
throughout the war, 121, 125,
128; fairly matched in first part
of war, 128; government shared
between, during peace of Nicias,
129; division of, based on regular
principles, 132

Politics, Athenian, importance and
difficulty of study of, 2; inadequacy and bias of original authorities on, 2, 3; old view of, 2;
Grote's view of, 3; present estimate, 3; no continuous history
of, 10; foreign politics more important than home, 24; false
theory of, 123 ff.

Population of Attica, at the beginning of the war, 40; numbers of
different classes of, 41; decline
of, owing to the war, 107

Πορισταί, 64 n. 2

Πρόβουλοι, appointed in 413, 16
n. 1, 96; not directly mentioned
by Thucydides, 64 n. 2

Προστάτης τοῦ δήμου, chief demagogue, 51; position of not official, 51; Grote's theory of, 52;
not "leader of the opposition,"
52; often held military command,
53; did not often take the field,

54; position open to, if also general, 54

Πρύτανις τῶν στρατηγῶν, theory of,
20; evidence for existence of, 21
n. 1, 22 nn., 23 nn.; importance
of office of, 24; combination of
powers of, with political influence, 55

Ψήφισμα, special weapon of the
demagogue, 62; 98 n. 2

Sicilian Expedition, The, advocated
by Alcibiades, 57; part of the
democratic policy, 77; motives
of Athenians in undertaking, 77;
cause of failure of, 78 n. 1; ex-
haustion of treasury consequent
on, 111; regarded as a commercial investment, 114; altered the
situation of Athens, 117; advocated by Alcibiades, 131

Socrates, and the Athenian Constitution, 80 n. 1; objection of, to
the lot, 96 n. 1

Sophists, The, and the Athenian
Constitution, 80 n. 1

Sparta, professions of, in undertaking the war, 27 n. 3; supports
oligarchs against Athens, 31 nn.
1, 2; objects of, in forcing on the
war, 33, 117; and Argos, 33, 76;
allied with Persia and Syracuse,
118; to blame for beginning the
war, 133

State Pay, importance of, exaggerated, 42, 45; condemned by
Aristophanes, 98

Themistocles, efforts of, to make
Athens a sea power, 14

Thera, Athens seeks to gain, 26, 72

Theramenes, probable treachery of,

CAMBRIDGE PRINTED BY C. J. CLAY, M.A. AND SONS, AT THE UNIVERSITY PRESS.

www.ingramcontent.com/pod-product-compliance
Lightning Source LLC
Chambersburg PA
CBHW030602270326
41927CB00007B/1010